THE TRAVELER'S GUIDE TO LOVE

A Memoir on Identity, Alignment, and Choosing Yourself

ZHARA YORK

Little Wild Experiences: A Journey of Risk, Culture, and SelfDiscovery by Zhara Michelle York

First Edition: 2026

Published by Little Wild Experiences Press

For inquiries, contact: info@littlewildexperiences.com

Disclaimer

This book is a memoir based on my lived experiences and personal reflections. All events are presented from my perspective as I understood and experienced them at the time.

To protect privacy, names, identifying details, timelines, and circumstances have been changed or intentionally obscured. Any resemblance to actual persons or events is coincidental and not intended as a literal or comprehensive portrayal of any individual.

This work is not meant to judge, diagnose, or define others. Its purpose is to explore identity, growth, and self-understanding through my own journey.

Acknowledgements

This book would not exist without my mother, Azaira G. Sanchez. May she rest in peace.

Whether consciously or not, she was the foundation of my values, my structure, and my inner compass. She was not a perfect woman — but she was a devoted mother, deeply present in the lives of her children, and unwavering in her respect for who I was becoming. She never asked me to be smaller, quieter, or more convenient. She honored my dreams even when they didn't follow familiar paths.

From her, I learned to treat family as something sacred — not impulsive, not casual, not accidental. I learned that love carries responsibility, that choices echo forward, and that building a life requires intention long before it requires compromise. That understanding shaped every major decision I made, even when it meant waiting longer, standing alone, or choosing restraint over immediacy.

Without her guidance, her example, and her respect for my independence, I would not be the woman I am today — a woman grounded in clarity, loyalty to herself, and deep reverence for the word family.

This book carries her influence in every chapter.

For that, and for everything else, I thank her.

How to read this book This book is not a manual.

It is not advice.

It is not a set of rules to adopt, defend, or argue with.

It is a lived record.

I wrote this book because for much of my life I felt lost in ways I could not easily explain. Not lost in direction, but lost in belonging. I often felt judged or displaced by friends, by relatives, and at times by the very people who claimed to love me. No matter where I stood, I sensed I existed just outside the frame others expected me to fit into.

Even then, something stayed steady. The way I am, the way I love, the way I move through the world is mine. It always has been. Still, there were moments when I questioned whether being myself required adjustment, whether parts of my identity needed softening or negotiation in order to be accepted.

I built my life from the ground up. From nothing. Everything I have, came through work, beginning early, without guarantees, without a safety net, and without the expectation of being carried. Along the way, people did help. They showed up at the right moments. But I never assumed my life would be held by anyone else. That responsibility became the center of who I am.

What follows is not a story of victimhood, nor a declaration of superiority. It is the record of a woman learning, through experience, what happens when you remain loyal to your identity even as the world asks you to dilute it.

This book is meant to be read slowly. Not as a linear romance, but as a mirror. Some chapters may feel familiar. Others may feel distant or uncomfortable. That discomfort is not an invitation to judge. It is an invitation to notice.

I do not believe there is one correct way to love. I do believe there is one correct way to love yourself, by knowing who you are and refusing to abandon that truth for attachment, approval, or fear of being alone.

What I call structure, sovereignty, and identity may resonate with you, or it may not. That is not a failure of this book. It is its function. Alignment does not require sameness. It requires clarity.

If you recognize yourself in these pages, take what belongs to you and leave the rest.
If you feel challenged, pause before resisting and ask why.

If none of this speaks to you, that is also information.

This book is not here to convince

It is here to illuminate.

Read it as a conversation, not a conclusion.

Read it with curiosity, not expectation.

Read it not to find love, but to understand the structure that allows love to last.

Introduction

I am a traveler by nature, an explorer, a why-not kind of woman with a passport in one hand and a journal in the other. Staying in one place for too long has never worked for me. I am pulled toward new perspectives, new cultures, new ways of seeing. But the journey that shaped everything that followed was never about geography. It was about love, and before anything else, learning how to love myself without abandoning who I am.

For years, that kind of self-love felt complicated. I often felt out of place, wondering why I couldn't settle into spaces where others seemed to belong so effortlessly. I forced myself into structures that were never designed for me, and the result was predictable, quiet dissatisfaction. Over time, I began to understand myself more clearly, and with that came a deeper understanding of why alignment matters more than comfort or approval.

It may sound self-centered at first, main character energy and all, but the truth is simple. If you don't understand yourself, honestly and without performance, you will never recognize who is meant to walk beside you. You are the compass. You are the reference point. Everything else orients around that.

Love feels like its own form of travel because life itself is a journey. Like any meaningful trip, it comes with detours, delays, missed connections, and emotional baggage you didn't plan to carry. We are not meant to move through it entirely alone. We crave connection, not for validation or spectacle, but for companionship. For someone who sees your worth and feels lucky simply sharing the seat next to you.

For me, love has never been only about connection. It has always been about structure, a form that cannot violate my identity. And my identity is not easily bent. I have spent much of my life alone, not lonely, but self-governed. I built my world early, and because of that, my sense of self became steady, grounded, and clear. That clarity created mismatches in my relationships, misalignments I didn't understand at the time but now see plainly.

For years, I questioned why I rejected men so easily, why affection, loyalty, effort, and even genuine care sometimes fell short. What I eventually recognized was that something essential was missing. I needed structure. I needed self-possession. I needed a partner who could stand beside me, not lean on me. Love, for me, has to support identity, not dissolve into it.

This story is personal, but it is not singular. You will likely recognize parts of yourself in it. Understanding who you are makes connection less mysterious and far less painful. Not everyone is meant to stay. Some people belong to a single chapter, a short season, or a moment that changes you and then passes. That impermanence does not lessen the value of the connection.

I am, unapologetically, a romantic. I believe in butterflies, late night conversations, electric first kisses, and goodbyes that linger long after the door closes. I also believe in knowing the difference between love and attachment. Attachment grips. Love moves freely. Once you learn that distinction, life becomes calmer and far more honest.

Travel gave me connection in unexpected forms, fleeting sparks, lasting friendships, and bonds that felt deeper than language. What surprised me was how consistent dating patterns were across borders. The scenery changed, the food changed, the customs changed, but the behaviors did not. We flirt, retreat, attach, disappear, open up, shut down. Everywhere I went, I saw the same rhythm, and eventually, I saw my own patterns reflected back at me.

Love is not only about who you meet. It is about what you bring into every connection. Dating taught me more than any classroom ever did. Some experiences strengthened my patience, others clarified my boundaries, a few tested my sense of reality, but all of them brought me closer to the kind of love I want to live inside.

When we fall for someone, we get intoxicated by possibility. Red flags fade under soft lighting. I know this because I've lived it, more than once. But everything returns to honesty, especially honesty with yourself. When you show up fully and without editing, you give others the chance to do the same. That is where connection becomes real.

In these pages, I share stories, romantic, absurd, tender, and funny. Stories gathered across borders and stories rooted at home. Each one is a fragment of my experience, offered without instruction. What you find in them is yours to notice.

Table of Content

Chapter 1

Where My Identity Was Born

Before I begin telling you the love stories, the beautiful ones, the chaotic ones, the ones that broke me open and rebuilt me, I have to start at the true beginning. Not with a boyfriend. Not with a country I traveled to. But with the woman who shaped everything in me, my mother. May she rest in peace.

For the early part of my childhood, I genuinely believed I had a stable family. My mother was a full-time housewife, the kind of woman who poured her entire being into raising her children. She cooked, read to me at night, helped with homework. Her world was motherhood, and she lived inside it completely. It was beautiful. And yet, it was not a structure that would ever fit me later in life.

My parents stayed together until I was five, maybe almost seven, and then came the first infidelity. I remember the moment I realized my family was not what I believed it to be. Around that time, I desperately wanted a little brother. My parents tried for one, and on the surface, life returned to something resembling normal. But the damage had already been done. The cracks were there, even if I could not yet name them.

Years later, when I was twelve or thirteen, a second infidelity surfaced. A classmate came over to work on a school project and said, casually, "I saw your dad holding hands with another woman." In that moment, the ground shifted beneath me. Not only because of the betrayal, but because it confirmed something my body had known long before my mind could articulate it. I went to my mother. She nodded. She had known. She had carried the truth quietly, protecting me from it as long as she could. But betrayals always find a way through.

I unraveled after that. I felt betrayed by the people who were supposed to be my foundation, so I detached. I spent time with relatives out of state, observing families that appeared stable, safe, financially secure, everything mine was not. And slowly, through that detachment, I formed the first layer of my identity, independence.

I loved my mother deeply. Her love was unconditional and consuming. I also witnessed her suffering. I saw a woman who loved fully but did not realize her marriage had already ended. I sided with her without question. I protected her pain. I rejected the new woman in my father's life. My brother and I lived divided, two lives cut cleanly in half. My father existed in one world without us and another with us.

Somewhere in the middle of all of this, I made a promise that became permanent. I would never bring a child into a fractured emotional system. Ever. I would not repeat what I had witnessed or build a life on hope instead of stability. I understood early that my needs as a person came first, not selfishly, but structurally. The partner I chose would have to be capable of building a life with me, not around me. Someone whose presence strengthened the ground beneath us instead of destabilizing it. I turned inward and built myself first, emotionally, financially, psychologically. I refused to create a family before creating myself.

Ironically, my mother reinforced this vision without realizing it. She used to say, "Make sure the man you choose to be the father of your child deserves that title." Those words rooted themselves in me. Over time, they evolved into what I now recognize as identity-based love, a framework few people ever learn, but one that saved me. It guided my decisions not toward perfection, but toward alignment. Toward becoming someone strong enough to stand alone and discerning enough to only stand beside someone who could match the life I was building.

By fifteen, I had stepped into adulthood. Not by choice, but by necessity. Instead of breaking, I built. I left home, left my mother, the person I loved most, and moved to another country. Distance did not weaken me. I created stability again, my own space, my own rules, my own world. Independence did not strip me. It crowned me. I became responsible for my life, my identity, my future.

Once a woman reaches that level of selfhood, she cannot allow someone else to destabilize it. That does not make my way superior. It makes it uncommon. Most people never form an identity strong enough to filter love through. They choose partners through emotion, timing, fear, or loneliness. I couldn't. My system rejected what did not align. Not because I was cold. Not because I was guarded. Because I was clear.

No chemistry, no comfort, no affection could override what my body already knew when something did not fit. Lifestyle, habits, emotional maturity, family dynamics, when they clashed with my foundation, I walked away. That was how I learned the difference between love and misalignment, between connection and structure, between feeling and identity.

When my mother passed away, the person I loved most in the world, and I learned about her death through a text message from my younger brother, something inside me fractured. I remember running out of a subway station in New York City, heading home from work as if speed could outrun grief. Even then, I did not fall apart in public. I held myself together until I reached my apartment. Only there, on the floor by the door, did I let myself break. I cried because I am human. But life did not stop. It kept moving. And somehow, so did I.

I did not attend her funeral. Not out of detachment, but out of protection. I refused to let my final image of her be reduced to a body instead of a presence. I chose to remember her as she lived, not as she ended. That choice taught me everything about boundaries and the preservation of the inner world.

So how could I ever accept a partner whose emotional life is scattered elsewhere. Someone fully enmeshed with others, divided in loyalty, presence, and attention. A romantic relationship, for me, is not a side arrangement. It is the beginning of the family I choose to build. It requires clarity, intention, and full alignment.

That is who I am. That is my structure.

My mother's teachings became a legacy I protect fiercely. I will not abandon them in the name of loving someone else. I honor them by loving myself.

This is the beginning of what I call Identity-Based Love. Every country, every relationship, every heartbreak circles back to this foundation.

Before we go further, one thing needs to be said clearly. Women who guard their identity, who walk away quickly, who choose themselves first, are often labeled traumatized. Their independence is mistaken for damage. But this is not trauma. This is standards. My identity did not shrink to survive my childhood. It expanded. It sharpened. I was not broken by what happened. I became the authority of my own life.

And that is the woman who begins this story.

Chapter 2

That Travel Revealed, What Love Confirmed

Love doesn't ask for a passport. It finds you where you are, sometimes across the street, sometimes across the world, and sometimes in places you never expected anything to grow.

Travel has always been part of who I am, but I never decided to date internationally. There was no plan, no experiment, no desire to collect stories across borders. Life simply placed people in my path, at home, abroad, in airports, cafés, on trains, and occasionally in places where love had no business appearing, but did anyway.

Some stories unfolded in New York. Others in Tennessee, Spain, Morocco, Rome, and places that felt temporary yet left lasting marks. Each connection revealed something about me I could not have seen on my own.

Dating across cultures changes you, and sometimes it is not even dating. It can be a conversation, a moment, a connection that stays long after it ends. The same is true within your own culture. When your surroundings shift, patterns become easier to see. A man in Nashville may show care through routine and courtesy. A man in Madrid may communicate interest through intensity and presence. In Italy, intimacy can live in small gestures. At home, love may be expressed through plans, goals, and practicality. Different expressions, same human pulse underneath.

And wherever I went, the constant was me.

For a long time, I believed the disconnects came from culture, language, expectations shaped by geography. Eventually, a different pattern emerged. The mismatch was never the country, the accent, or the customs. It was structure.

Some men offered affection. Others offered passion. Some brought consistency. A few offered fantasy. Almost none offered the alignment my identity requires for love to exist at all. It did not matter where they were from. If a man lacked sovereignty, if his emotional life was scattered, if he blurred boundaries that needed clarity, if he needed guidance instead of standing independently, emotionally and financially, the attraction faded. Not because I am cold, but because my identity does not contort to fit what does not belong to me.

Still, there was beauty in those connections. Sitting across from someone whose life looks nothing like yours, yet whose presence feels real, is powerful. Even when the moment is brief. Even when the story is not meant to last. Even when a translation app does half the work. Whether in Nashville or Napoli, love speaks the same language, curiosity, desire, possibility, and the quiet fear of repeating familiar mistakes.

Travel taught me this early. New scenery does not erase old patterns. A new country does not resolve misalignment. Novelty does not create structure. Whatever you carry inside yourself comes with you until you are willing to face it.

Mine did.

There were times I chased intensity instead of stability. Times I chose mystery over clarity. Times I let attraction override intuition because the moment felt too beautiful to interrupt. Every connection, whether it lasted a night, a week, or a season, became information. Not analytical, not detached, but the kind of knowing that forms when you pay attention to your own responses.

It took years to understand that many people are not struggling to find the right person. They are struggling to understand themselves. They change cities, apps, countries, partners, believing the next place will feel different. Without identity, the outcome repeats. Different faces, different settings, the same confusion. Until you know what makes you feel grounded and safe, love will remain unclear. Until you define your non negotiables, attraction will keep pretending to be alignment.

I am not a psychologist. I am a woman who noticed patterns. I learned that love, for me, is not a feeling. It is a structure. My identity is not movable furniture. It is the foundation. And the right man, anywhere in the world, speaks the same language, presence, clarity, sovereignty, emotional responsibility.

Travel expanded my world. Love clarified my structure. Together, they taught me something simple and often overlooked, connection can cross borders, alignment cannot.

Every man I met, every country I entered, every romance or almost romance pointed me back to myself. The stories I carry, beautiful, chaotic, heartbreaking, joyful, did not teach me how to love someone else first. They taught me how to love myself without losing myself.

Chapter 3

The Bridges That Built Me

Before we move through the love stories scattered across continents, we have to return to where it all truly started. And it did not begin in Rome or Paris or under some poetic foreign sky.

It began in a noisy cybercafé in Venezuela.

The kind inside a mall, where you paid by the hour, where keyboards clicked constantly, where teenagers typed to strangers across the world. Long before swiping existed, there were AOL chat rooms, dial up tones, and connection speeds that depended entirely on whether someone at home decided to pick up the landline.

That is where I met Mateo.

I was fourteen. Rebellious and unsupervised in the very specific way children of distracted, divorcing parents often are. He charmed me through screens, through calls that lasted too long, through gifts that felt too grown up for my age, and through a confidence my teenage self-mistook for maturity.

He even managed to charm my mother. Not in a malicious way. He never harmed me. But this was not something a child should have been involved in, even if it later shaped the woman I became.

Before long, I had built fantasies around him. Wedding venues in Venezuela. Futures I was not old enough to articulate, let alone understand. Life moved quickly after that. My parents divorced, and my mother signed paperwork allowing me to travel with my father to Florida, where his family lived. We stayed there for a few months. Later, my father signed another document so I could travel alone to New York.

My independence began early. I was already trying to create my own world, my own sense of family. When we arrived in Florida, my father eventually moved to Tennessee, predictable for a musician. I went in the opposite direction, to New York, to Mateo.

And the moment I saw him, truly saw him, I knew I did not want him.

But what does a teenager know about love. At that age, love meant intensity. Messages. Phone calls. Being wanted. I did not understand the difference between connection and escape, between attachment and admiration, between desire and direction.

Mateo was not my soulmate. He was my exit. A way out of the emotional aftermath of my parents' divorce. A way out of a life that felt too small for what I sensed inside myself. He was a bridge to something else. And bridges are not meant to be homes.

Within weeks, we moved to Long Island. My father went one way, to Tennessee. I went the other, toward independence, toward a life I had imagined long before I had words for it.

That is where love truly began for me, in New York City.

Not romance, but awareness.

I felt awake. I knew I wanted something different, even if I did not yet know how to build it. I understood that I would have to create my own safety, my own home, my own sense of stability. I knew patterns would repeat unless I stopped them. I knew I had to build myself first.

Even then, before I could articulate it, I understood something clearly. My family would be me and whoever I intentionally chose to build a life with later. No one else. I could not return to the place I had left, the place that had destabilized me completely. I did not know when I would see my mother again. I did not know when I would see my father again. My brother was much younger than me, and we had not yet formed the bond I longed for.

That was the moment reality became unavoidable. From that point on, it was me. Just me. And everything I would build would come from that truth.

Mateo and I lived together for two years, though the relationship had ended the moment I arrived. We stayed in a small room rented from his relatives, a space that always felt temporary. Little by little, I realized he was not the person I wanted to build a life with. The truth was simpler and deeper. I wanted to be with myself. I had dreams, ambition, a fire that did not match his pace. My body understood this long before my mind could explain it.

I drifted emotionally, and later physically. Not out of malice. Not out of confusion. I already understood the ending, even if I did not yet have the language to close it properly. Eventually, I left. That moment marked the true beginning of my life on my own.

I rented a room in Manhattan, my first place that felt genuinely mine. During those final months with Mateo, I traveled to Manhattan once a week for modeling school. Each trip felt like breathing into a different version of myself. The city revealed possibilities I did not know existed, and in doing so, exposed just how misaligned we truly were. New York activated parts of me that could not survive inside resignation.

Years later, Mateo reached out, looking for closure or nostalgia or something I never cared to define. I did not feel the need to reopen that chapter. Some chapters ask only to be acknowledged, not revisited.

New York brought new people quickly. Ronald and Rick.

Ronald was the son of the woman who rented me my first room. Rick was a regular at the bar where I bartended. I was sixteen, far too young to be living like an adult, yet already doing exactly that. As for how I worked so young, I learned early how to make my own way.

I was fond of Ronald. But Rick was different.

I fell hard, or what my sixteen-year-old mind believed was falling in love. Rick was divorced, though that concept meant very little to me at the time. Marriage and divorce felt like adult language I did not yet understand. What I felt was safety. He felt present. He wanted me, or at least that is how it felt, and I wanted him.

Years later, I understood that he was another bridge. He showed me how easily need can be mistaken for love, and attachment for alignment.

I worked odd jobs. I survived. He let me stay in his Brooklyn apartment. I grew attached for the wrong reasons. I felt protected, but protection was never enough.

When I lost my job at the bar, his offer of a place to stay felt like stability. For a teenage girl who had left her country, her mother, her childhood, it felt like home. It was not.

I did not yet have the emotional structure for partnership. I mistook dependency for intimacy. I mistook intensity for love. I mistook proximity for safety.

Then I became pregnant.

I was seventeen. Still a child myself. I had to make a decision no teenager should have to make. It was the right decision for me.

I was not ready to be a mother. I was not ready for a life I did not choose. I was not willing to repeat the chaos I came from. I was not willing to abandon my path, even for love that looked like protection.

After that, the relationship unraveled. I was immature, insecure, searching for something I could not name. Rick ended it. The heartbreak was devastating. In confusion, I moved closer to him, believing proximity could fix what misalignment had already decided. It could not.

Years later, he reached out again. By then, his life had unfolded in ways that confirmed everything I already knew. We met once. I closed the door. Some doors exist for a reason.

He was not the one. He was a step.

What I did not know then, but understand clearly now, is that none of these relationships were failures. They were foundations. Mateo taught me that escape is not love. Ronald taught me that connection alone is not enough. Rick taught me that protection is not partnership.

I did not have the language back then. I do now.

My independence was instinct, not rebellion. My choices were clarity before vocabulary. I was not avoiding commitment. I was protecting a sense of self that was already forming. I did not break. I built.

And that identity, strong and unmistakably mine, would determine every love that followed.

Chapter 4.

How I Would Never Again Be

My breakup with Rick was devastating. It took almost a year to truly move past him. As time passed, the sharpness softened, slowly and unevenly, but it did fade. I was working in catering then, moving through weddings, graduations, anniversaries. The weddings were the hardest. They stirred a longing I did not yet have language for. I remember one in New Jersey, the city glowing across the water. I could see New York in the distance, my New York, and I remember imagining that one day I would be the bride in a scene like that, not the server quietly circulating with trays.

During that period, I was not dating, but I did spend time with people I met through work. Not recklessly, but out of loneliness. Those moments were distractions from the absence Rick left behind. I remember going for drinks after a shift with a Colombian coworker. One night became another, and then it ended. It was not meaningful. It was never meant to be. I was searching for relief, not connection. I was eighteen, still living in a rented room, trying to find footing in a city where my own apartment felt impossibly far away.

One day, while sorting through my things, I found Ronald's phone number. He was the son of the woman who had rented me that room years earlier, someone I had met while I was still with Rick. I called him without much thought. We reconnected easily. He had liked me back then, but I stopped speaking to him when I became involved with Rick.

Looking back, I know I used Ronald as an exit. A rebound. At the time, it felt natural. I was young. I had plans. I believed relationships were about companionship, missing someone, needing someone. It would take years to recognize how often I repeated that pattern.

What I had with Ronald existed somewhere between necessity and comfort. I needed stability, and what we shared fit into my life the way survival decisions often do. I understood, even then, that it was a passage rather than a destination. A chapter meant to move me forward, not one meant to last.

I knew he was not my lifelong partner, but I also knew I needed to be there at that moment, in that version of my life. There was no intention to hurt or manipulate anyone. I was not calculating outcomes. I was doing the best I could with the awareness I had.

My focus was survival, direction, and building a future I could eventually stand on. My goals came first. They had to. For a long time, I called that selfishness. With time and clarity, I understand it as self-preservation. If you are not grounded, you cannot offer healthy love.

I chose myself not out of disregard for others, but out of responsibility for who I was becoming. I protected my future so that one day, when I did love, it would come from stability rather than survival.

Eventually, Ronald and I married at City Hall in New York City. One morning, no ceremony, no planning. We walked in and did it. I do not think his family even knew at first. We lived with his parents for a while, but I knew we needed our own space. I have always needed a home that feels safe and intentional, a place where growth is possible.

Ronald had lived with his parents his entire life. He worked odd jobs, had no defined profession, and moved at a pace different from mine. He was not a bad man. His life simply did not align with the structure I needed. His mother was deeply involved in his life, protective in ways that felt parental rather than empowering. That closeness did not fit the partnership I envisioned. After our divorce, he returned to their home, confirming what I had sensed early on. It was not a flaw. It was a different structure.

I found us an apartment. Once we moved in, tensions surfaced, rooted less in anything I had done and more in emotional insecurity. He supported me in ways I will always acknowledge, but he was also dealing with unresolved internal struggles. At times, those struggles appeared through mood shifts, emotional instability, and the role alcohol played in certain moments. I did not judge him. But I understood I could not live in an environment where steadiness was inconsistent. Care and gratitude could not replace stability.

I knew I had to leave. There was no explosion. Just a quiet knowing that staying would mean betraying myself. I found another room and began disentangling my life. Even then, I sensed the story had not fully closed.

Before distance became final, I became pregnant again. It became my second and final abortion. The decision was not rushed. It stayed with me. It deepened my understanding of responsibility and consequence.

Much later, I would learn that I could never carry children, not because of those decisions, but because of something entirely unrelated.

At that moment, I knew with certainty that Ronald was not someone I could choose as the father of my children, not biologically, but structurally. I was the adult in the relationship. I understood permanence. I understood that children bind you to another person for life, not temporarily, but through decades. I was not willing to create that bond without alignment.

For me, having a child has never been about desire alone. It has always been about permanence. About shared futures. About choosing carefully who remains in your life forever.

That clarity became foundational. From that point on, I became deeply protective of my structure. Identity must be honored. We live with ourselves forever. Betraying that truth carries consequences.

Ronald was not that person. Recognizing that was not rejection. It was responsibility. It was also the moment I understood that choosing not to have children can be as intentional as choosing to have them.

That realization came with force one day in the subway when I fainted. I was pregnant again. The decision was immediate. Not out of fear, but necessity.

What followed was darker. During one of his emotional spirals, he lost control. We struggled over a knife. He was intoxicated and disconnected from reality. I was trying to protect myself. The blade pierced my chest. The injury was superficial, but blood is blood, and trauma is trauma. The police arrived quickly. The scene spoke for itself.

There had already been many arguments before that night. I was young and unprepared to handle conflict the way I can now. And yes, at one point, he raped me. When consent is absent, even in marriage, it is rape. I stayed silent to avoid escalation. Silence felt safer then.

After the incident, he was handcuffed in front of me. I stood outside in my pajamas giving my statement. The next day, the district attorney contacted me. A temporary order of protection was issued. The state wanted to press charges. I did not want destruction. I wanted distance. I wanted peace.

Later, after I moved again, he appeared at my door. I must have shared my address earlier, never imagining danger. I never saw him as a threat. But the encounter ended the same way, jealousy, accusations, chaos. That was confirmation. It was over.

Years later, he reached out online. Maybe he wanted closure. Maybe memory softened the truth. I responded kindly. There was nothing more to say. Some stories end long before the final page.

Chapter 5

When Standards Become Your Shield

After my first divorce from Ronald, I spent seven years single. Seven years building myself quietly, even when I didn't yet have the language to describe what I was doing. I was still in school, juggling classes and life, and little by little, I began to travel more. At first, it was just short trips around Latin America—quick escapes, small glimpses of a bigger world. But somewhere along the way, I fell in love with traveling. Every new place, every language, every culture unlocked something in me. It felt as if the world was introducing me to versions of myself, I hadn't met yet.

During those seven years, I still craved a relationship—not out of desperation, but because I was raised with the belief that family was sacred. My mother taught me standards long before I fully understood what that meant. She would say, *"The father of your children must earn that title. It is a privilege."* Those words stayed in my bloodstream. They became the baseline for everything I later expected.

But the world is filled with characters. Not everyone sees family, commitment, or stability through the same lens. And for me—for me—the love of my life was always inseparable from the father of my child. Whoever that man would be, he had to be aligned. He had to deserve the architecture I intended to build.

I dated during those years. And no one met the standards.

I kept encountering men who wanted pleasure, distraction, fantasy—anything but structure. Some were financially unstable. Some were emotionally chaotic. Some simply weren't wired for what I wanted. It was exhausting. And without realizing it, my heart began breaking in tiny pieces—silently, gradually, painfully.

In New York, before I had the language for any of this, I went out with a man—young, unstable, already carrying the weight of a fractured family and unresolved responsibilities. At the time, I didn't analyze it. I didn't diagnose it. I only felt the familiar pull: the quiet expectation that I would once again compensate, stabilize, adjust myself around someone else's unfinished life.

Looking back now, I see it clearly for what it was—not a failure, not a step backward, but a test. One of the first moments where life placed the pattern directly in front of me and asked, *Do you see it yet?*

Even then, before exhaustion turned into clarity, I could feel the truth in my body. Every time I met someone, there was something to fix, something to manage, something that required me to bend or become smaller so the relationship could function. And although I didn't yet have the strength or the vocabulary to stop it immediately, the lesson was already forming.

You cannot change people. You cannot mold someone into your standards. You cannot sculpt a partner out of misalignment. Love is not a renovation project, and partnership is not an act of rescue.

I didn't fail that test—I simply hadn't finished learning how to read it yet.

Still, I became attached. And then reality revealed itself in the clearest way possible: he stole money from me.

The humiliation was immediate. The pain was real. I was devastated—not just by the theft, but by the fantasy I had constructed in my own mind. I had believed love could exist where values didn't align. That

I called my mother. She didn't lecture me. She didn't judge me. She simply said, *"I didn't raise you to be weak. I raised you to rise. To be independent and strong. Nobody can break you. Move on."*

And that was all I needed.

I moved on.

But something in me hardened. I placed my dreams of love in a box, locked it, and threw the key somewhere I never intended to retrieve. From that point on, I dated without purpose—not for love, not even for hope, but for company. For attention. To feel alive in episodes.

I became emotionally detached.

Please me, because you are not enough to earn a place in my life.

That became the unspoken rule.

Financial instability?

Lack of alignment?

No structure?

Not fit to build a family?

Disqualified.

My standards were high—not out of arrogance, but out of clarity. I wanted a family that belonged to me and my future partner, and none of these men had what it took.

Before all the random dates, there were a few men who touched me in smaller ways—men who taught me lessons even if they were never meant to stay. During my undergraduate years, I worked in hospitality: hostess, waitress, bartender, and sometimes even on-call manager, mostly in upscale French restaurants. That's where I fell in love with wine and with elegance itself.

I worked at a French restaurant on the Upper East Side—charming, refined, not fully upscale, but beautiful. I was the hostess. That job came through a sous-chef I had worked with earlier, during the transition between Rick and Ronald. That's when I met Nate.

Nate was Algerian—multilingual, cultured, magnetic. I've always been drawn to Algerians, perhaps because of their languages, their depth, or my own love for the world. He caught my attention slowly. Everything began when the staff would go out for drinks at the Japanese bar next door after a shift. That's when I fell in love with sake. We went as a group—the waiters, the bartenders—and Nate and I naturally gravitated toward each other.

Soon enough, we slipped into a situation ship.

Too much physical attraction.

Too much chemistry.

Too much, *almost* wrapped in the wrong structure.

I felt excited every time he called or texted, yet deep inside I already knew the truth: this man was not for me. He was a waiter, and there is nothing wrong with that—I was one myself. But for my personal and professional standards, he didn't fit. I always knew I could explore, experience, and learn—but my real love, my foundation, my future family had to be saved for someone aligned with my architecture. Nate wasn't him.

Then there was Nelson—Nate's French friend. Elegant, attractive, refined. My type. He approached me first, even before Nate. We exchanged numbers. We went out. I liked him. I saw potential. But again, commitment was absent. He was a gentleman—but unavailable.

The last time I went to his place, he was tense, angry about something unrelated to me. He desired me physically, but his presence was hollow. I left the next morning knowing that the chapter had ended. And briefly, I drifted back toward Nate—not out of hope, but familiarity.

Eventually, I left the restaurant, and distance did what clarity had already begun. Nate and I faded—gradually, naturally. Years later, I heard he wasn't doing well. It broke my heart in a quiet way. I wish him well, sincerely. He was never meant to stay, but he mattered in a fragment of my life.

Those years taught me something essential:

Attention is not affection.

Desire is not commitment.

Chemistry is not architecture.

That season became my shield.

The season where my standards—buried but intact—protected me.

The season where I learned that not every man fits the life you are meant to build.

And that forcing it only breaks you in the process.

Chapter 6

The Season I Learned to Control Attachment

After I left the French restaurant, I found a job as a waitress at a steakhouse in Spanish Harlem. That's where I met Victor. Without realizing it, he became my long-term situationship—my long-term distraction, really. He worked in the kitchen, and he lived upstairs in the apartments the restaurant owners—two brothers—owned. Later, I learned he had some sort of business arrangement with them. At the time, he was just another employee to me, but eventually, things became more complicated with that family… including an affair with one of the owners. That comes later. For now, there was Victor.

I can't even tell you how many years that situationship lasted—long enough to feel like a shadow-life. At the time, I was working two restaurant jobs while attending school full-time. I was exhausted on every level: physically, emotionally, spiritually. Victor became a pause from all of it. He was easy to talk to, grounded in his presence, uncomplicated. We would spend hours talking, and intimacy followed—not as an end in itself, but as part of the closeness of those moments. What I became attached to wasn't the physicality, but the simplicity of it being just us in that space. No past. No future. No demands. A suspended world where nothing was required of me.

But again, he didn't fit my architecture.

He didn't have the drive, the ambition, the elegance, or the alignment I knew I needed to build the life I dreamed of. And realistically, he wasn't in a position to commit either. I hadn't awakened anything serious in him, and I didn't try to. My clarity was there, even when my attachment blurred it.

We slowly faded. Less talking. Less seeing each other. Life is pulling us apart. Neither of us is fully available. That's how some chapters close—not with drama, but with silence.

Ironically, that was also the period when one of the brothers—the restaurant owners—invited me out for the night. It wasn't intimate or suggestive; it was a group outing that blurred business and nightlife. At one point, we stopped briefly to collect money someone owed him, then continued on. By the end of the night, intimacy happened once—impulsive, detached, and without emotional weight. The following work shift, we spoke as we always did, as if nothing had occurred. No tension. No discomfort. Moments like that teach you something subtle but lasting: that physical connection can exist without meaning, that chemistry doesn't always signal direction, and that not every encounter is a story meant to continue.

Another night, he invited me out again, this time with friends. Among them was a man I didn't find attractive, yet something in me had already shifted. I was exhausted—tired of being unseen, tired of offering depth where none was received, tired of giving my full presence only to feel invisible. That night, I didn't act from desire; I acted from awareness. I allowed attention without attachment, engagement without illusion. I understood what I was doing, and I understood why. It wasn't cruelty or manipulation; it was distance. It was control. It was the realization that I no longer needed to merge emotionally to survive a moment.

Looking back, it may sound cold. But at the time, it wasn't emptiness—it was armor. It was the moment I learned that access to me could be measured, that intimacy didn't have to cost me my center, and that I could choose who entered my emotional world and who never would. I wasn't becoming hardened; I was becoming intentional. I wasn't losing my values; I was learning how to protect them.

Time passed, and something unexpected happened. This is what I previously mentioned. Rick found me online. My first love—the man who left a lasting imprint on my emotional memory. Social media was just beginning then, and one day his name appeared with a friend request. I accepted it without much thought. We spoke casually at first, the way people do when too much history sits beneath the surface to be acknowledged all at once.

One day, I posted that I wanted to watch a scary movie at the theater and asked if anyone wanted to join me. Rick replied. After six or seven years of no contact, that was how I saw him again. We watched the movie, and afterward I took him to one of my favorite places—A restaurant near Columbia University. It was a familiar setting for me, a place I had shared with different people over the years, including Victor.

Ironically, years earlier, I had tried to find Victor online. He didn't have social media, but someone with the same first and last name, the same age, and a strangely similar background appeared instead. I joked about it at the time and even arranged for the two of them to meet once at the café. It was awkward, almost surreal, and oddly revealing. I think, in hindsight, I just wanted to see the real Victor clearly one more time.

Later, when my connection with Victor had already begun to dissolve, I allowed myself a brief, inconsequential encounter with that resemblance. It wasn't desire or longing—it was closure in disguise, a quiet confirmation that nothing there could replace what was already gone.

But Rick was different.

After the movie and a quiet drink, carried by the familiar nostalgia that surfaces when two people share unfinished history, we returned to my apartment on the Upper West Side. What followed felt less like a beginning and more like an echo of something unresolved. The next morning, we walked through the park, speaking easily, like people who had never fully closed their chapter. And then, as before, he disappeared again.

He had built another life. He had children. And that realization hit me with a familiar sharpness.

We once had a relationship. I got pregnant. But we never wrote that story—not because love wasn't present, but because alignment wasn't. He didn't rise to the standards required to build a family with me, and he knew it. We could have created a life from zero, but he didn't choose me—not then, not in the way that mattered. And the truth is, I wasn't ready either. I wasn't prepared for a relationship back then, much less for building a family. Deep inside, I already understood that timing without structure is just chaos wearing hope's clothing. Some doors don't need to be slammed; they just need to be closed with intention.

Life is ironic like that. Men return to rare women. Misalignment returns as memory. But clarity—clarity stays.

Chapter 7

When Familiarity Felt Like Destiny

I kept going. I kept moving alone, the only way I knew how. Independence had become my safest place—the one structure no one had ever managed to shake for me. During this time, I reconnected online with an old classmate from middle and high school. Armando. Another reconnection in a season full of digital reunions, back when Facebook was still new, and everyone was resurfacing from childhood.

He and I were never close growing up. He belonged to the popular crowd—the soccer-playing, always-surrounded-by-girls type. And I was the introverted, nerdy girl with glasses, quietly watching the world from the margins. I never saw him as anything more than a classmate.

But life is ironic. Years later, both of our families had randomly ended up in the United States—his in Tennessee, mine partly in Tennessee because my father lived there. He was in Memphis; my dad was in Nashville. Somehow, that became a bridge between us. We started talking, reminiscing about school, our childhood, and how much had changed.

Then one day, he told me he was in New York.

He didn't plan it. He didn't set a date. He simply called me while I was standing outside my school between classes and said, "I just arrived in New York." I remember the rush of excitement—not romantic excitement, but the sweetness of having someone from my childhood suddenly appear in the city that had become my world. New York was my home now, my adult life, my new universe—and seeing someone from my past step into it felt surreal and beautiful.

I told him we could meet for drinks after work. I finished class, went to my job, then ran home to change. He sent me an address near the Alphabet City area. He was there with a friend from Memphis—let's call him Jose. When I arrived, I met them all. They were staying with another friend, and we spent the night laughing, drinking, and dancing.

That night, I met Venezuelans for the first time in years. It didn't awaken a sense of culture or belonging, but it did stir something familiar in me. They reminded me of a version of myself from long ago—a younger chapter I had almost forgotten. It felt strangely comforting to have people from my past life standing in the middle of the life I had built in New York.

The next day, we explored the city together. I let my spontaneous spirit lead us from place to place. Bar hopping, new conversations, new connections. At one bar, I struck up a conversation with the bartender—or maybe the owner, I don't remember now—but he took to us immediately and invited us to another spot after he closed. We went. We danced. We stayed up far too late.

And somehow, at the end of the night, all of us ended up sleeping in my bed. Not romantically—just human exhaustion thrown into a small New York room. At that time, I didn't have an apartment, just a single room with a bed that suddenly had more people on it than it was ever designed for. It was chaotic and innocent at the same time, one of those nights where youthful energy replaces logic.

A strange little moment of humor, freedom, and adventure—New York in its purest form.

Somewhere in all of that, something shifted between me and Armando.

I don't know when it happened, but before he flew back to Memphis, we were all riding in a cab. When it came time for me to get out, he leaned in and kissed me—soft, quick, gentle. And I froze. My mind started spinning. *Wait... he's just a friend. A classmate. How is this happening? How do I feel something for someone I never saw that way? And he's not even my type.* But something in that kiss stayed with me. I kept thinking about it.

After he returned to Memphis, I grew close to Reina, the Venezuelan girl Jose was seeing. We became girlfriends quickly, and she wanted to visit the guys. She encouraged me to explore things with Armando—though I think her main motivation was seeing Jose again. But we were young, adventurous, craving connection. So we planned a trip.

We stayed at Jose's house, and almost immediately, Armando and I grew closer. He introduced me to his family—his mother, his cousin, his uncle—and they welcomed me with a warmth that felt sincere and unforced. For the first time, I could sense what it might be like to begin a story cleanly, without baggage or inherited complications, without shadows from the past—just two people who shared a childhood context, standing at the edge of something new. His family offered me everything I had always imagined a beginning should hold: acceptance, simplicity, and a quiet sense of belonging.

Armando fit in a way that felt effortless. His structure mirrored mine. His background was uncomplicated, his family intact, his goals aligned with the direction I was moving in. We understood each other without needing long explanations or emotional negotiations. It felt as though what I had been waiting for—without ever fully being able to name it—might finally be taking shape. At the time, I didn't yet have the clarity to articulate what I was choosing or why, but looking back, it is obvious: even unconsciously, I was always choosing structure, alignment, and cleanliness of origin. I knew what I wanted long before I knew how to define it.

And then reality intervened.

Armando was preparing to leave, entering a new phase of his life. The night before his departure, we shared an intimacy that felt both tender and final. I stayed with him, and earlier that evening, I had taken his family out to dinner, paying for everyone as a quiet gesture of gratitude for how warmly they had welcomed me. Later, as we sat in the car before returning to his place, he turned toward me and said—

"Zhara, you intimidate men."

That sentence stayed with me for years. At the time, I didn't fully understand it. It lingered quietly, resurfacing at different stages of my life, until experience gave it meaning. What he had sensed— what I would later come to articulate—was that I had always been deeply independent. I never chased. I stayed faithful to my principles. I moved through life with a quiet certainty about what I wanted: structure, clarity, and the intention to build a family from zero as the first and only woman in a man's life. I was never going to repeat my parents' story, and any man who chose me would have to protect that same sacredness with the same devotion.

We returned to his house and became intimate again. Somewhere beneath my logic, my subconscious hoped for something—a sentence, a promise, a thread to hold onto. But nothing came. He didn't say, "Let's figure this out." He didn't ask to stay in touch. He simply continued toward the life he was choosing, and I moved toward mine.

I returned to New York heartbroken—not because he was the love of my life, but because he embodied the structure I wanted, and for a moment, I believed timing might bend in our favor. It didn't. We weren't aligned. We weren't in sync. Our destinations did not match.

Still, like most humans, I tried. Reina wanted to see Jose again, and I knew Armando would be in Memphis visiting family, so we planned a second trip. We drove overnight in a caravan of five or six cars, stopping at bars along the way, sleeping in the car while rain tapped against the windows. We went to the lake, rode a jet ski, and lived the way youth does—loudly, freely, without filters.

But Armando wasn't there.

I swallowed my disappointment and kept smiling, but I had hoped to see him. When we returned to Memphis for a house party, he finally appeared—and that's when I learned he had a girlfriend.

The realization hit instantly. I remember thinking, *Wait—I thought he wasn't looking for anything. I thought he was focused on moving. I thought timing was the issue.* But the truth revealed itself with brutal simplicity: if a man wants you, nothing will stop him; if he doesn't, everything will.

He had moved on, and I needed to do the same.

I blocked him everywhere—not out of bitterness, but out of clarity. When I close a chapter, I close it fully. That is how I survive. That is how I grow.

Years later, we reconnected briefly online—nothing deep, just a quiet acknowledgment that we still existed in the world. I learned he had a child, a life, a path entirely separates from mine. He wasn't the one. But he left me with something important.

Not every man who fits your blueprint is meant to build your architecture. Timing, alignment, and identity matter just as much as compatibility.

Armando was a beautiful almost—a clean beginning that was never meant to become a life. A chapter that shaped me without needing to continue.

Chapter 8

The Men Who Taught Me What Structure Really Means

After the heartbreak with Armando, I kept moving through my life in New York City. I dated a few men here and there, nothing meaningful, nothing that touched the deeper parts of who I was. Life, however, had its own way of reconnecting paths. Back in Memphis, where I had met so many mutual acquaintances, some of our friends were Cuban—big personalities, lively spirits. One of them, Harry, became close with Reina and me. Another, Robert, Armando's friend's brother, also became part of our little circle. They visited us in New York sometime later, and for a while we fell into a rhythm of easy friendship, long nights, and the kind of carefree moments that only exist in your twenties.

Harry had a cousin, Tom. One afternoon, I called Harry for help with something legal, and he mentioned Tom might know more. Harry put us in touch. At first, the conversations were purely informational, but Tom told me he would be traveling to New York soon, and maybe we could catch up. I didn't see anything wrong with that. When he arrived, we met, talked, and bonded—another harmless connection in a long chain of temporary ones. Eventually, we became sexually involved, though I didn't want anything serious. I wasn't physically attracted to him in a meaningful way. He was simply another episode in a period of my life marked by fleeting interactions. I liked attention; he provided it.

At one point, we even took a road trip to Florida together. For me, it was entertainment—a distraction from my routine and a way to fill the emotional gaps between who I was and who I was becoming. For him, it clearly meant more, but I wasn't interested in turning it into anything significant. When we returned, I told him the truth. He was sweet, but this was not going anywhere. And just like that, another chapter ended.

As I continued meeting these men, I realized I wasn't lost or confused—I was filtering. I didn't yet have complete clarity about what I wanted, but I had absolute certainty about what I would not accept. I didn't want a financially unstable man; I had worked too hard to build my independence. I didn't want someone without ambition; I had always been entrepreneurial and driven. I didn't want an insecure man; I was grounded and confident in myself. And most importantly, I needed a man with structure—personal, emotional, and familial. I needed to be the woman he chose deliberately for the best chapter of his life, not an addition to an existing story. That was non-negotiable.

Somewhere in this process, I realized something essential: I wasn't falling in love with men. I was falling in love with structure—the architecture of a life where I could be the chosen one, the origin of a family built from zero. That realization explained far more of my past than I understood at the time and planted the seeds for why I believe I never had a family of my own later. But that belongs to another chapter.

For now, this is where Caleb enters my life.

Caleb was one of the most important men I ever met. We worked together at a major transportation company in New York. He had an extraordinarily pure heart. After seven years of shallow relationships and disappointing encounters, he arrived offering sincerity, affection, and emotional steadiness. He cared for me in a genuine way, gave me space in his life, and learned me deeply — my patterns, my reactions, my values, my boundaries. He understood who I was becoming and who I was not meant to choose. He wasn't someone life had shaped me to avoid; he was someone who reminded me what real intention looked like.

He was gentle and loving, and that tenderness drew me in. It made me fall in love with him in a way that felt safe and sincere. But he came with a past—a family—and by now you understand how deeply that conflicted with my internal architecture. It wasn't that having a past was wrong; it never was. What made it incompatible was that his circumstances collided directly with the foundation I had spent my entire life protecting.

I had always envisioned myself as the first, the origin—the woman a man consciously chose to build a family with from zero. I wanted to be part of the beginning, not an addition to an already complex structure. That distinction mattered to me more than I knew how to articulate at the time. Caleb couldn't offer me that then, and I didn't fully understand why it unsettled me so deeply. I only knew something felt misaligned, even though the love was real.

So, we tried. And in time, he did something remarkable: he offered me the structure I had always preserved and protected. He didn't do it out of obligation or sacrifice, but out of understanding—because he wanted to meet me where my identity lived. At the time, that felt like enough. And for a while, it was.

And then my world broke again.

In our second year together, my mother passed away—the day after her birthday, August 15, 2012. She was the only woman who had ever truly understood me, the one who protected me emotionally without trying to change me. Losing her fractured something inside me, something I still carry. During the holidays that followed, grief consumed me quietly but completely. Work became overwhelming, life felt unmanageable, and Caleb and I tried—honestly tried—to support each other through it all.

But the unresolved dynamics from his past—lingering entanglements, emotional noise, worlds that could not truly blend— began to seep into our relationship. Not out of malice on his part, but because some structures simply collide when they are not designed to coexist. For me, it became emotionally suffocating.

Then came the accident.

One chaotic day at work, I drove a truck to help Caleb unload his own. New electric trucks were being tested, and as I pulled in behind him, the brakes failed. My truck hit him, pinning him between the vehicles. I froze. I don't remember getting out of the truck or running. I only remember finding myself inside a nearby store, the manager—who knew me—trying to shield me from the police and paramedics. My mother had just died, and at that moment, I believed I had killed the man I loved.

I fainted.

At the hospital, I was confined to the psychiatric ward for hours. I couldn't speak. I couldn't move. All I wanted was to call my mother and see Caleb. My mother was gone. Caleb was in surgery.

When I was finally released, I was taken to the hospital where he had been transferred. His family was there. His entire world was there—the ex, the child, the history, the complexity. And there I was, grieving, traumatized, emotionally depleted, barely holding myself together. I tried to be present for him, but I could hardly function. I lost weight rapidly. I slept most of the day. The medications prescribed to stabilize me only made things worse. I was unraveling.

Eventually, Caleb did the only thing that could have freed us both: he asked me to leave.

He told me, *"You should live the life you deserve."*

It shattered me. He was the most loving man I had ever known, and I loved him deeply. But I also understood why he did it. At the time, he knew he was about to enter a long and uncertain therapeutic process, one that would demand all of him, with no clear timeline for recovery. Later, he explained that his decision wasn't about pushing me away—it was about not tying me to a version of himself that could not fully show up for me. He didn't want me anchored to someone who, in that moment, couldn't offer the presence, stability, and wholeness I deserved. And as painful as it was, I knew he was right. Our structures were fundamentally incompatible, and staying would have meant betraying who I was and the values I had spent my life protecting.

I had finished my undergraduate degree and had nothing anchoring me to New York anymore except memories and heartbreak. So, I left. I searched for work overseas and accepted a job in China, moving thousands of miles away because I needed distance to breathe again.

In China, I felt free. Nothing reminded me of the pain—not my mother's death, not Caleb, not the emotional spirals I had barely survived. I traveled extensively across Asia. I met people. I lived.

I formed a connection with a younger coworker—someone who, by his own admission, had little experience with intimacy. We began studying together for the GRE, and our breaks turned into conversations, which eventually turned physical. It wasn't love. It was an escape. He wanted to experience closeness; I wanted to feel desired enough to forget.

Later, I briefly dated a Chinese man from a privileged background. The mismatch was obvious from the beginning. It didn't last, and neither of us sought anything meaningful. Just another moment between two people passing through each other's lives, each needing something temporary.

Throughout all of this, Caleb never truly disappeared. He emailed. He called. He stayed present in his own gentle way. And I missed him, too. The men I met abroad wanted fleeting pleasure; the ones who wanted commitment lacked the structure I needed. Caleb—despite a past that didn't align with my blueprint—offered an emotional stability I wasn't finding anywhere else.

He never abandoned any responsibility. That was never the story.

What he understood—intuitively—was my architecture. He recognized how I build connection: with clarity, intention, and clean structure. Out of respect for who I am, he organized our space in a way that honored my identity. Not to fix anything in me, but to meet me where I had always lived.

He didn't erase his life. He created boundaries. He separated worlds—not out of denial, but out of understanding. He gave our connection a space where it could exist on its own, uncomplicated and dignified. And that effort—*that* respect for the way I love—is what created the bond between us.

Whether that approach was right or wrong is not for me, or anyone else, to judge. I never asked him to change. I stepped away when things didn't align, and he adjusted only in the ways he chose to. What mattered was the intention: he understood my emotional architecture and responded with sincerity.

For almost a year, we stayed in contact while I lived in China. I never returned home during those two years.

Then one day, he appeared in the lobby of my apartment building in Beijing. He had mentioned he might come, but I didn't believe it until I saw him standing there with his luggage. During our time apart, he had sent flowers, gifts, and messages filled with commitment. He respected my world. He protected my peace. He tried—genuinely—to align his life with mine.

But some circumstances cannot be erased.

I had to travel to Hong Kong to renew my work permit, and that time away became an opportunity for reflection. He stayed in my apartment with my dog. While in Hong Kong, I met people and had a brief, insignificant encounter—so insignificant I don't even remember the man's name. It wasn't betrayal. It was uncertainty. It was me trying to understand whether returning to Caleb was the right choice.

Two years later, Caleb saw messages from that man on my phone—harmless group invitations, nothing romantic. Still, jealousy surfaced, and his reaction shifted something irreparably. The truth was, I already had one foot out of the relationship. Even though he had worked to protect my emotional world, I still didn't belong within the larger structure surrounding him. And it wasn't fair to either of us.

I returned to the United States. He followed a couple of weeks later, hoping to mend what was breaking, but he couldn't let go of the Hong Kong incident—not even the name I had already forgotten. That was the moment I knew I had to start over again.

We lasted a few more months, but the misalignment became impossible to ignore. This time, it wasn't about structure—it was about ambition, vision, and financial direction. Our paths were simply moving at different speeds, toward different horizons. And although Caleb always found a way to reappear in my life, I had come to understand something essential: some love stories are not meant to stay with us. They are meant to shape us, refine us, and prepare us for what comes next.

He was the man who loved me most beautifully on an emotional level, yet the man whose life could never fully align with mine in the places that mattered just as much—ambition, direction, and financial stability.

His story does not end here. There is another chapter for Caleb— because eventually, he became my husband and one of the most significant figures in my life. He gave me structure. He adjusted his world to protect my peace. He loved me with sincerity.

But alignment requires pillars. And when even one is missing, the foundation cannot hold.

In his case, the missing pillar was financial stability.

And that, as you'll soon see, shaped everything that came next.

Chapter 9

The Standards That Became My Compass

Once I believed things with Caleb were truly over—or at least that is what I thought at the time—I tried to move forward again. I was single once more, still searching for affection, still craving connection, but always anchored in my professional goals. It felt as if I was waiting for a man whose life moved in sync with mine: someone career-driven, emotionally disciplined, a man who was also waiting for the right partner so he wouldn't taint his love story with the wrong one. I imagined a man who was saving himself the way I had been saving myself, someone who understood timing and intention, someone who valued a clean beginning as deeply as I did.

But this was also the chapter where I made one of the biggest mistakes of my life—trying to adjust my identity to what the universe delivered instead of calibrating my path to stay aligned with who I truly was. Adjustment violates identity. Calibration protects it. I didn't know that yet, and I betrayed myself more times than I care to admit. Still, I kept walking toward my goals, protecting the dreams I hadn't achieved yet. Until I built the life I wanted, nothing personal could move forward—unless the right man arrived to add to that vision, not distract from it.

During this period, I worked at a language center in Queens, teaching English to adults. It was the position I took immediately after returning from China. That's where I met a colleague—another teacher—and, almost without intention, we began spending time together. I can't pinpoint exactly when it became something more, but before I realized it, I was being introduced to his parents, his brother, his sister-in-law. He showed me family values, a kind of structure that quietly reminded me of Armando. There was intention there, seriousness, a genuine openness to commitment.

What drew me in wasn't romantic intensity—it was the idea of what he represented. His family was warm and welcoming, and I appreciated how naturally they embraced me. There was comfort in that environment, a sense of order and belonging. But as time passed, the misalignment became clear. He wasn't financially stable, and ambition—the kind that mirrors long-term vision and personal drive—was missing. While the family structure existed, the forward momentum I needed in a partner did not.

He wanted a serious relationship, and his intentions were sincere. But intention alone is never enough when the foundations don't align. I knew, quietly and early, that I couldn't build a future there. Letting him go wasn't a rejection of who he was; it was an acknowledgment of who I am. He tried to make it work, but I understood that forcing alignment would only lead us both to disappointment. Ending it was the only honest choice.

Around that time, I transferred from Queens to the Manhattan location of the same school. That's where I met Daniel. It started with casual conversations during breaks, which turned into drinks after work. Eventually, one night after a few drinks, he kissed me right in front of the subway entrance by Madison Square Garden. I liked him. He was younger, but something about him pulled me in. Still, the connection lacked depth. He dragged the situationship the way these men often do—lingering long enough to keep you emotionally available but never committing. Conversations that should have built substance instead fell flat. His personality felt… off somehow, almost mismatched with mine. Yet attraction carried things further than they should have gone.

Eventually, I noticed him giving more attention to a new teacher at work. It was subtle, but I wasn't stupid—I could feel the shift. Around that time, I resigned from the school after receiving a better job offer. Later, social media confirmed what my intuition already knew: he was engaged to that teacher. Our connection had never been serious, but it was something, and I always wondered why he kept me orbiting around him if he knew he wouldn't choose me.

Life moved on. I left the country again, and our communication faded. When I later saw news of his engagement—an engagement that didn't last—I disconnected from all his social media. Still, Daniel somehow found his way back to me. He reached out, and we reconnected lightly as friends. Even during my years abroad, he would message me from time to time, usually asking about how to find work overseas. We shared a love of travel, and that kept a gentle thread between us.

Years later, when we met in person again, he casually mentioned a relationship he had been in. I knew exactly who he meant—the same teacher he became engaged to after things were unclear with me—and clearly, they were no longer together. I didn't comment; there was no need. His path had taken him elsewhere, and honestly, him choosing differently had been for the best.

After some time on my own, I eventually decided to seek therapy. I had been carrying the weight of my mother's death in silence, and her absence left a deep wound I hadn't fully faced. I missed her dearly. She shaped every value I held: my standards, my expectations of love, the sacredness of family. She taught me that children are not accidents, that choosing the father of your children is a privilege that must be earned, not given lightly. After she passed, those standards—already firm—became even more sacred. They became her legacy.

But gosh, grieving my mother's death took time—real time. And in that process, I learned something profound: when you lose someone you love with your entire being, someone who shaped your identity, someone whose presence grounded your world, you don't "get over" it. You simply learn to live with it. Especially for someone like me— someone who loves without clinging, who loves without bending identity, who loves without needing physical closeness—grief becomes a private space you inhabit quietly. The memory of that person becomes a permanent room inside you.

This is true not only for mothers or siblings or the family members we naturally associate with loss. It's about significance—the impact a person creates in your life. You can feel this even with someone you once loved romantically, someone you knew was not meant for you, yet whose presence carved itself into your emotional architecture so deeply that no matter where life takes you or who comes afterward, that person remains inside you like a tattoo. A mark that doesn't fade, even as you keep moving forward.

But we will talk more about this later.

During that period, everything felt blurry. I was grieving, trying to navigate life without her grounding presence, and I didn't realize then that I had begun bending the very standards I had promised myself to protect. My subconscious knew it—my identity sensed it—but my conscious mind hadn't yet caught up. That clarity would only come much later.

During one therapy session, my therapist asked whether it would be helpful to bring Caleb into the sessions. I wasn't sure what to think of that. I said yes, but deep inside, I didn't know if it would help— or if anything could have helped at that time. I didn't understand myself then the way I understand myself now. And so, slowly, quietly, almost without awareness, I started again—convincing myself that getting back with Caleb might be the right thing to do. He offered sincere and pure love. He respected my space, my boundaries, and he gave me the emotional structure my identity needed. But something was always missing. I didn't know then what exactly it was, but I learned that later.

Chapter 10

When Love Is Not Enough Without Architecture

When I reached out to Caleb again, he accepted without hesitation. Nothing made him happier than the idea of trying one more time. We entered couples therapy, and in that process, we became closer than ever. Caleb was, at that point in my life, the only man who had ever truly learned me—learned the way I think, the way I love, the way I protect myself, the way my identity operates. He understood my standards, my structure, my emotional architecture. He adjusted to me naturally, not because I demanded it, but because he intuitively sensed what my peace required. His circumstances allowed him to create the emotional space I needed, and for a while, that was enough.

Years later, after we moved from New York to Nashville, I suggested he invite his son to the home we had built together. For me, this mattered because by then we had a stable structure—a kingdom of our own. I have always believed that when a relationship is grounded in true architecture, nothing threatens it. The foundation defines everything: who is the core, who orbits, who enters, and under what terms. That clarity is not jealousy or immaturity; it is logic, organization, and emotional hierarchy. Families thrive when roles are defined, when partnership is the axis, and when every other relationship or connection orbits respectfully around that center. That is the version of family I always envisioned—clean, intentional, and free of chaos—and that is the structure I have always loved.

But before reaching that clarity, life had taken us through many phases. For the second time in our relationship, I stepped away. Distance was always my reset button—the way I recalibrated when something no longer aligned with my identity. During that separation, a moment of misalignment made it clear that I had drifted from the version of myself I expected to be inside a relationship. When integrity slips, even momentarily, that is my sign that I cannot stay. It was never about another person; it was about recognizing that if I crossed a boundary I had always honored, then emotionally I was already gone. Caleb understood this with a compassion only he was capable of offering. Even when we created distance, our connection never truly disappeared; it softened, it shifted, but it never broke.

Caleb gave me structure and knew how to align with me without losing himself. Alignment can come afterward, but only if the changes one person makes are changes, they would still choose even if they were single. For Caleb, these changes were not about compromising; they were about evolution. I activated an identity in him that already existed. I didn't force anything—I was simply the catalyst. He didn't adapt; he restructured. He aligned to start the life he always wanted with the woman he loved. For him, it was happiness, not sacrifice. And for that, I will always love him.

However, Caleb was a very laid-back person and lacked financial drive and ambition. That is not wrong, but it didn't align with mine, and that can become an issue when it touches the foundation, which it did. I knew it. I knew it was a piece of my identity that had to be present in a relationship, and those are non-negotiable for me. So I decided, again, that this had to end, or at least that is what I thought at the time.

After we separated that second time, I moved to Dubai. Life unfolded naturally there, quietly and without expectation. I met people from different backgrounds, and while each connection reflected a moment in time, none aligned with what I was seeking. I wasn't chasing entertainment or attention; I was observing architecture. I wanted to know whether a man existed whose ambition, emotional discipline, and internal structure matched mine. What I encountered instead were individuals moving through life without clarity, without commitment, and without a grounded intention to build something meaningful.

In that contrast, one truth became unmistakably clear: even with our imperfections, Caleb was the only man who had ever offered the emotional structure that aligned with my identity. He understood me in a way that felt rare—deep, precise, and enduring—even from a distance. I understand now why I kept returning to him. Finding acceptance within a shared structure felt far rarer than building financial stability, and for a long time, I believed I could compensate for what was missing, that I could support, guide, and help carry the weight. But over time, that dynamic became unsustainable. What begins as devotion eventually becomes exhaustion when alignment is incomplete.

Two years overseas passed, and I returned to the United States. We found our way back to each other—not out of fear or desperation, but out of familiarity, shared history, and quiet understanding. He suggested moving to Nashville to be closer to my parents. Leaving New York felt like abandoning a piece of myself, but buying a home there was nearly impossible; the prices were high, and the taxes felt like a punishment for loving my own city. Still, owning my own home had always been a dream. Nashville made sense financially, logistically, and practically, even if, emotionally, I wished I could have stayed in New York. So, we moved.

We lived together in Nashville for two years, building what appeared to be a stable life. But beneath the surface, the alignment was quietly breaking. I wanted to build a business, to create something of my own with long-term purpose, and Caleb wasn't meeting me there. His financial life was disorganized, and eventually, undisclosed financial issues surfaced—debts, secrets, patterns of instability that destabilized the foundation I had tried so hard to build. I found myself carrying the entire financial structure of our life—bank calls, accounts, payments, savings, investments— everything. I controlled everything because he wouldn't, and that was the misalignment. For a woman like me, whose identity is anchored in clarity, ambition, and independence, that imbalance became impossible to ignore.

But before Nashville, before Dubai, before any relocation became a reset, we lasted years together in New York City, in the apartment I kept until I moved to Nashville. But before moving to Nashville something very deep happened during those years—something that shook me in a way I never expected. I went to see my doctor and found out I had cancerous cells in my cervix. That news made me spiral. The first thought I had was of my mother, because coincidentally, she died from cervical cancer, even though doctors later explained that her situation had nothing to do with mine.

I remember the day I was told. I was sitting in the doctor's office, and I couldn't move. It was a panic attack. Everything felt urgent. It was clear I needed surgery quickly, and I was scheduled for the procedure. I had a LEEP—Loop Electrosurgical Excision Procedure—a procedure where cancerous cells are removed. I tried to breathe through it. I tried to convince myself it would be enough.

Then I went to the follow-up appointment, like you normally do after a procedure, and I was told I needed to see an oncologist. I remember thinking, *What? Seriously? Why would I need an oncologist?* They weren't clear. They tried to calm me down and told me I simply needed to see the specialist. But those days— waiting—were torture. I was trapped inside my own mind, imagining possibilities I didn't want to imagine.

When I finally saw the oncologist, the truth landed: the cancerous cells came back. I had to proceed with a hysterectomy. The doctor wasn't happy about doing it because I was young, late twenties, early thirties. She decided to do a partial hysterectomy, so I would still have the option to conceive through a surrogate mother if I wanted to, but it turned out that the process is long and stressful. And the truth was simple: it was either that, or risk my life.

I knew I wasn't ready to have children at that time, and I wasn't even sure if I would ever be ready, because my structure honestly didn't allow it without alignment. But what pained me was that the decision was made for me. Not by me. Life decided. Circumstance decided. My body decided. And I had to live with that.

Caleb was there throughout the entire process, and he was there even after my mother passed—he was still there even when things fell apart. There were many moments when he was by my side. That man was, and still is, a beautiful soul.

I was his priority. He contained our relationship and did not allow anything or anybody to disturb me emotionally. Anything that would cause me emotional pain, destabilize me, or shake my peace, he would not allow. And that—without losing himself—was one of the most beautiful gestures a man has ever done for me for true love. He did it because it made him happy. He was happy with me, and that mattered to me.

And that is what makes this chapter complex. Because the end was not about the absence of love. Love existed. Respect existed. Care existed. Structure existed in many ways. But for women like me who seek alignment, love is not one pillar. Structure is not one pillar. A relationship needs multiple pillars, and if one pillar is consistently missing, the architecture eventually collapses. Our last two years in Nashville were becoming the end.

Ending the relationship wasn't a decision of emotion; it was a decision of structure. Financial alignment was missing, and without all pillars, the foundation cracks. Staying would have meant betraying myself. So, I ended it—not impulsively, not out of rage, but out of clarity. And clarity hurts, especially when the person sharing life with you has been good to you.

When the relationship ended, it felt like losing a friend more than losing a partner. In the quiet of my mind, I remember asking myself who would ever learn me the way he had. I know that sounds selfish, but it was honest. Being understood that deeply is rare. I mourned him quietly, and at the time of writing this book, I think a part of me still does. But mourning doesn't mean regret. It means honoring what was.

I grew with Caleb; we grew together. When we met, my identity was already clear, but I didn't yet know where I belonged. I expressed my true self to him in ways that were still immature—not because I didn't know who I was, but because I was young and still trying to understand why I didn't fit in certain places, why I reacted so strongly to overlapping histories, to unresolved chapters, to the presence of lives that were not meant to remain active in a partnership meant to build forward.

Caleb was the man who, without realizing it and without judgment, showed me that I was far more clear than I had ever given myself credit for. At the time, my standards felt unreasonable even to me, and I punished myself for needing what I needed. Yet through him, I began to see that my clarity was not rigidity—it was instinct. I wasn't rejecting people; I was protecting the center of the life I was trying to build.

For me, love has always required a clean emotional landscape—one where the past is acknowledged but no longer active in the present. That understanding didn't come all at once, but it was already there, quietly guiding me, long before I had the language to name it.There is one truth that will remain with me forever: Caleb is the only man in my life who has earned my true respect. I will always care for him—not romantically, but in a respectful, gentle, and genuine way—because he left a positive impact on me, and he knows that. Our story didn't last, but the impact did. And that is something I will always honor.

We ended things clearly and honestly. We accepted our fate. We moved forward separately, each carrying what the relationship gave us. I stepped into my new chapter with peace in my heart, grateful for what he represented and wishing him nothing but the absolute best.

And yet, there was a truth I hadn't fully learned at the time: sometimes the most dangerous chapters are not the ones that break you loudly, but the ones that blur you quietly. When love ends without chaos, when the person wasn't "bad," when the relationship wasn't "toxic," you don't leave with anger—you leave with grief, and grief can make identity foggy.

Looking back, I understand something I couldn't articulate then. I wasn't rejecting people, and I wasn't afraid of love. I was protecting the center of my life—the place where my identity, my future, and my peace had to remain intact. Once I understood that, I stopped apologizing for the way I chose. Some people are meant to walk beside you for a season; others are meant to teach you where your boundaries live. Both can matter. Only one can stay.

That is where the next chapter begins.

Chapter 11

When Identity Goes Quiet, Illusion Speaks Louder

After my divorce from Caleb, I wasn't angry. I wasn't dramatic. I wasn't even broken. I was grieving—quietly, internally, without spectacle. Grief without chaos is the most disorienting kind because there is nothing obvious to rebel against. There was no villain, no betrayal that justified rage, no single moment I could point to and say *this is why*. Love had existed. Care had existed. Safety had existed. And yet, something essential had still been missing.

When a relationship ends not because it was destructive but because it was misaligned, you don't leave with certainty. You leave with questions. You leave with a strange emptiness that doesn't come from loneliness, but from the realization that you gave years of your life to something that could not fully meet you. That kind of ending forces you inward. And that is where I found myself—alone with my thoughts, my identity, and the quiet fear that maybe I still hadn't arrived where I thought I had.

I told myself I was ready to move on. I believed I was strong enough, clear enough, detached enough. But in truth, my identity had not fully settled yet. I was in transition—emotionally, professionally, existentially. I had left a marriage that mattered, a life that had structure, and a man who had known me deeply. And even when the decision is right, the nervous system still needs time to recalibrate.

This is something people rarely talk about: how leaving a relationship that wasn't wrong can make you more vulnerable than leaving one that was. There is no anger to protect you. No story to hide behind. Only the quiet work of rebuilding yourself while the world assumes you are "fine."

That is when identity can go quiet.

And when identity goes quiet, illusion speaks louder.

I moved forward believing I was simply opening myself back up to life. In reality, I was trying to grieve by creating a new life too quickly. I didn't want to feel what I was feeling. I wanted to be clean of pain, untouched by it, already on the other side.

And here is the truth no one prepares you for: it is easy to leave a relationship when it is wrong, when there is damage, betrayal, or chaos to justify the exit. But when there is no damage—when the love is real, the respect intact, and the only reason you leave is loyalty to your own identity—that kind of departure hurts in a way that cuts deeper.

I needed immediate anesthesia, and I reached for it without fully realizing what I was doing. But anesthesia is temporary. It numbs without healing, distracts without resolving.

On the surface, my life looked expansive, open, and in motion. Internally, though, I was still reorganizing myself—quietly, invisibly, piece by piece. And when you are in that state of internal reorganization, even the smallest connections can feel larger than they are, simply because you are still finding your center again.

That is when I met someone through circumstance rather than intention. There was no attraction at first, no spark, no desire. It began with proximity, then conversation, then availability. Kindness entered the space, and kindness—when you are in transition—can be deceptively powerful. It feels safe. It feels grounding. And without realizing it, boundaries begin to soften.

I wasn't chasing love. I wasn't looking for romance. I wasn't even looking for companionship in the traditional sense. I was looking for stability without naming it. And when you don't name what you are actually seeking, you allow substitutes to enter.

What formed wasn't a relationship. It was a pause. A distraction. A temporary relief from the work of sitting alone with unanswered questions. I didn't fall in love—I drifted. And drifting is dangerous when identity hasn't fully anchored itself yet.

The truth revealed itself quickly. Integrity was missing. Structure was absent. The situation could not sustain real life, real partnership, or real alignment. And what I felt in that moment was not heartbreak. It was disorientation—a sharp, grounding realization that I had momentarily stepped outside myself.

What I mourned wasn't him

It wasn't the connection.

It wasn't the ending.

It was the idea I had briefly allowed myself to believe in.

The fantasy

The projection.

The imagined version of stability that had nothing to do with reality.

That moment was sobering, not devastating. Because deep down, my identity never disappeared—it had simply been quiet. And the second the truth surfaced, it returned fully, decisively, without negotiation.

This chapter is not about that person. It is about me. About how even a woman who knows herself deeply can momentarily lose clarity when grief, transition, ambition, and loneliness overlap. Vulnerability does not mean weakness. But vulnerability without grounding opens the door to illusion.

I walked away cleanly. Quietly. Without explanation. There was no need for confrontation, no need to educate, no need to justify my decision. When identity comes back online, it does not argue—it exists.

And the relief that followed was immediate.

Not relief from pain, but relief from distortion.

That was the moment I understood the lesson fully.

You cannot find the right person while you are still reorganizing yourself.
You cannot choose alignment while your identity is still settling.
And you cannot build real love from a place of emotional fog.

Real love is not urgency.

It is not attention.

It is not a distraction.

Real love is clarity.

And clarity exists only when you are fully present within yourself.

This chapter taught me something fundamental: relationships do not define me. Identity does. And when identity is strong, nothing misaligned can stay for long. You become impossible to confuse, impossible to manipulate, and impossible to pull away from yourself.

The lesson was never about someone else.

It was about the discipline of returning to myself—again and again—until who I am and how I live finally spoke the same language.

And once that alignment returned, I knew one thing with absolute certainty:

I would never again confuse presence with partnership, kindness with compatibility, or illusion with love.

What I didn't know then was that this wouldn't be the only time vulnerability would test me. This was the quiet version—the subtle one, the kind that slips in unnoticed when you are grieving and rebuilding. The next lesson would arrive louder, faster, and with higher stakes. That one would require not just awareness, but action. This chapter was about noticing when identity goes quiet. The next would teach me what happens when identity must defend itself.

Chapter 12

The Lessons We Meet in Vulnerability

When I ended my marriage with Caleb, I entered a period of mourning far deeper than I expected. I wasn't just losing a partner; I was losing the only person who had ever learned me so deeply, the only one who had walked beside me through so many versions of myself. The grief came in waves—quiet, heavy, unannounced. I asked myself questions I had asked before at different stages of my life: *Who will stand by my side now? What comes next? What if the rest of my life is just me?* And for a moment, I accepted that possibility with peace. I knew I had survived alone before. I knew how to build from zero. That strength had never left me.

But grief makes us vulnerable, and vulnerability makes us inconsistent. In that emotional fog, I made a mistake. I started dating again through an online app before even understanding what I wanted or what I was capable of giving. My heart was wounded, my identity blurred, and my vision clouded by the aftermath of ending something that had been real—imperfect, but real. Looking back, I know I was trying to fill an emptiness too quickly. I was searching for a distraction instead of direction. And that is the most dangerous place from which to invite someone into your life, especially after leaving a long relationship, not because love was absent, but because the misalignment was too deep and too fundamental for identity to sustain.

When you walk away from a partnership of years, you don't need company.
You need space.

Space to breathe.

Space to return to yourself.

Space to regain the clarity that alignment requires.

I didn't give myself the space I needed, and that is how I crossed paths with Dylan. Even now, writing about this chapter of my life carries discomfort. Not because of who he was, but because of who I was at that moment. This was the greatest emotional misstep of my life — not rooted in malice or illusion, but in my own unguarded vulnerability.

He entered my life with intensity, with overwhelming attention, with a kind of affection that felt consuming rather than grounding. At the time, I experienced it as love. Only later did I understand that what feels expansive when you are wounded can, in fact, be attachment amplified by timing. My mistake was not recognizing the difference.

Vulnerability does that. It invites us to project what we long for onto what is merely present. We don't see what stands in front of us — we see what we hope it could become.

He arrived during a season when my identity was softened by grief, and in that emotional disorientation, I allowed someone access to a part of my world that should have remained protected. His presence revealed misalignment almost immediately—not through dramatic conflict, but through absence: the absence of structure, intention, emotional grounding, and coherence with the life I was building. Nothing about the connection reflected my values.

Vulnerability has a way of making fantasy feel safer than reality, and for a brief moment, I tolerated what I would normally have declined without hesitation. That pause was not confusion about who I am, but a momentary distance from myself.

Very quickly, I felt overwhelmed by a dynamic that lacked emotional steadiness and clear boundaries. The rhythm between us felt erratic to me, and I noticed how easily I began to lose my sense of space. What we had started to feel more symbolic than lived — as though the relationship existed more as an idea than as something grounded in responsibility and presence. When he proposed, I realized with surprising calm that nothing inside me was aligned with that future. I wasn't choosing him; I was moving within the emotional current of my grief, allowing a story that did not belong to my identity to carry me forward.

He didn't meet me where I was, and I felt myself responding to an image rather than a grounded reality. Over time, the connection became draining — not because of cruelty or malice, but because inconsistency and blurred attachment slowly eroded my clarity. I found myself engaging with a version of the relationship that could not sustain itself without my emotional effort.

There were aspects of his life that seemed more visible than integrated, as if being seen could substitute for being settled. That never threatened my sense of self, but it revealed a fundamental difference in how we understood boundaries. I do not confuse proximity with connection, nor presence with alignment.

Eventually, the truth became undeniable: this was not a relationship rooted in mutual structure, but one sustained by my willingness to carry more than my share of the emotional weight. My vulnerability allowed the door to open, but it did not allow it to stay open for long.

I wasn't rejecting people. I was protecting the center of my life.

Boundaries are not punishments. They are information.

And once that information was clear, there was nothing left to debate.

This chapter is not about him.

He is irrelevant to the architecture of my life.

This chapter is about me.

About what I sensed.

About what I ignored.

About how vulnerability distorted my perception and how clarity eventually returned.

My instincts whispered warnings from the beginning, but grief blurred my intuition. Many people stay in situations like this for years, slowly losing themselves. The only reason I didn't is because, even at my weakest, my identity remained intact beneath the surface. It simply took longer for that strength to rise into my conscious awareness.

When clarity arrived, it arrived sharply. The cut was clean—no emotional negotiations, no drawn-out explanations, no space for rebuttal. Just a firm, final boundary. Lines had been crossed, and I chose myself. What drained me was not the other person; it was the fact that I had bent my identity, even slightly. I am not designed to merge into misalignment. I am not built to adapt to chaos. I am not meant to shrink to fit into someone else's unresolved life.

And so I walked away—clean, quiet, direct.

The moment I left, I felt relief. Freedom. Exhaustion, yes—but liberation.

I needed a reset. And for me, travel has always been the purest form of reset — an internal cleansing disguised as movement. I took myself to North Africa and Western Europe for two months, moving lightly, deliberately, and on my own terms. I have always known how to travel beautifully with very little. Those weeks gave me breath again. I met people from all over the world — some stayed, some didn't — but every interaction revived the part of me that had been suffocating inside misalignment.

Travel teaches you your own strength. It reveals the parts of yourself you forget while trying to love others. It reminds you that identity always returns when given space.

During those months, I understood something fundamental about why I was still alone. It wasn't because the right person doesn't exist. It was because I could not love outside of alignment. I filter; I don't date blindly. The right person is not found through randomness or emotional desperation. They appear when alignment appears:

Values.

Lifestyles.

Beliefs.

Identity.

Emotional rhythm.

Structure.

The right person doesn't create doubt, anxiety, or noise. Your body knows. Your nervous system knows. The right person feels like home—not a moment, not chemistry, not desire, not fantasy. *Home.*

I began to observe how often people build relationships out of circumstance rather than intention. Some couples move fast or face unexpected life events and still build strong partnerships because they grow into alignment. Others drift into roles without knowing themselves or each other, and misalignment appears—not because love failed, but because identity was never explored.

Foundational questions matter:

Do our values align?

Do our emotional rhythms match?

Do we handle stress compatibly?

Do we want the same future?

What is the core of my life, and what is the core of yours?

Do our identities complement each other, or will one collapse to sustain the other?

When alignment is missing, people adjust themselves or compromise parts that should remain intact. Sometimes that works. Often, it turns into resentment. For me, the truth was clear: I cannot love through the compromise of identity. My architecture requires clarity.

Looking back, I no longer see that chapter as a mistake. I see a mirror.

Every moment reflected something I needed to understand about myself—my boundaries, my emotional rhythm, my structure, and the conditions under which my identity thrives.

Healing doesn't happen when life is calm. It happens when life shakes you hard enough that pretending is no longer possible. Vulnerability exposes where we abandon ourselves. Misalignment shows where we bend too far. Heartbreak reveals the parts of us still waiting to be chosen—by us.

The lesson became simple, though not easy:

When you know who you are, you stop entertaining what isn't aligned.
When you honor your values, chemistry no longer confuses you.
When you respect your emotional rhythm, chaos stops feeling like passion.
When clarity returns, you stop tolerating anything that dulls your identity.

Love is clarity.

Alignment is non-negotiable.

Identity is the compass.

Emotional safety is a standard, not a luxury.

I walked away not because I was cold, but because I finally returned to myself.

My identity, once blurred by grief, became sharp again.

The lesson was never about others.

It was always—always—about me.

Chapter 13

When the World Gives You Back to Yourself

When I ended things with Dylan, I knew I needed a reset. I thought it would be the reset I had already needed after my divorce from Caleb. I believed that chapter had exhausted its lessons, that the grief had been processed, that the wound had closed. But for reasons I didn't yet understand, that wasn't the case. Life had one more chapter to add—one more mirror to hold up—before I could truly return to myself.

As human beings, we persist relentlessly in the search for love. We imagine the right person wearing the wrong costume. We project possibility onto availability. We confuse timing with destiny. And sometimes, we don't realize we're repeating a pattern until the repetition becomes undeniable.

So, when the nightmare chapter with Dylan ended, I didn't hesitate. I booked a two-month backpacking trip through Morocco and Western Europe. That was exactly what I needed—not to escape, but to recalibrate. To return to the parts of myself that had always been intact. To remember what fulfills me, what grounds me, what restores my sense of wholeness.

Travel has always been that for me.

I crave the unknown. I crave movement. I crave observing the world from different angles, listening to different languages, and learning how people live, love, and survive outside the framework I know. I don't need permanence in a place. I don't need roots in soil. I don't even call many places home.

There is one exception.

New York City.

But even that didn't become home because of family, history, or nostalgia. It became home because I built myself there. I wasn't born there. My relatives weren't there. There was no inherited safety net waiting for me. When most people think of home, they think of parents, siblings, cousins, childhood schools, and shared memories. That definition never fit me.

For people like me—independent, sovereign, whole—home is not inherited. Home is constructed.

I moved to New York City at an age when childhood dissolves into adulthood, when identity is still forming, but instinct already knows what it will not tolerate. I had no relatives there, no family support, no familiar structure. And that wasn't an accident. It was a choice. My blood family had shown me a structure I did not accept, and rather than replicate it, I chose distance so I could design my own.

And I did.

But back to the reset.

As I moved through Morocco and Europe, I met people from everywhere. Travelers. Locals. Drifters. Anchors. Brief connections. Fleeting conversations. Most of them were exactly that—moments that passed without imprint. But there was one person I met who stood out in a different way.

His name was Maurice.

He hosted travelers in Morocco, and I became one of his guests. From the beginning, his hospitality was sincere, generous, and deeply human. He welcomed people not as transactions, but as experiences. And after everything I had been through, that alone felt grounding.

I want to be clear about something: I wasn't looking for romance. This was not a dating app encounter. This was not a search for connection. I met him through a traveler's platform, something many people might consider risky, but when you've been traveling for a long time, you learn how to move through the world with awareness, discernment, and self-protection.

We started talking before I ever arrived. Long conversations. Real conversations. The kind that unfold slowly and honestly, without expectation. I spoke to him from Spain. From Italy. Those were my first two stops before Morocco. By the time I arrived, we already knew each other—not deeply, but genuinely.

The airport I landed in was far from his town, so I took a bus to the nearest station. That's where we met in person for the first time. He hosted me, and for almost a month, life felt gentle. We spent nearly every day together. He showed me his town, the surrounding villages, and the rhythms of daily life. It was simple. Grounded. Present.

Somewhere along the way, the conversations softened. The energy shifted. There had been light flirting even before we met, but one day, in private, he leaned in and kissed me. And that was the beginning.

What mattered most to me during that time was my clarity. I knew this wasn't going anywhere. I knew I was passing through his life. I was a traveler, not a destination. And yet, there was a connection— a real connection. The kind that exists even when both people understand the ending.

That is the paradox of these encounters.

You can imagine a future while knowing it isn't real. You can feel something deeply without mistaking it for permanence. And that is where I began to notice something important—something my body had been doing for years before my mind caught up.

Even in something temporary, I was observing structure.

We connected. We missed each other when we were apart. We saw each other every day. And then reality stepped in—sharply.

Morocco is a Muslim country. Religion shapes not just culture, but law. And as a Western woman with no religious affiliation, I felt the contrast immediately. There was one night in Marrakech that crystallized everything. I had rented an apartment. He came over. And in the middle of what could have been an intimate, romantic evening, he stopped.

He panicked.

He insisted he couldn't stay. He said people would talk. That the police could be called. That it would become a problem.

I knew the law. I had spoken to the landlord myself. He could have stayed for one night. There were ways around it. I had done my research. But fear isn't logical—it's cultural, internalized, inherited. So, he left.

I was left alone in that apartment, not heartbroken, but suddenly clear. Clear about the limits of fantasy. Clear about the difference between desire and alignment. Clear about how culture, structure, and internal freedom shape behavior.

We talked later. He apologized. He explained. I understood. But understanding doesn't erase impact.

Before I left Morocco, he took me to a local beach. We sat there staring at the ocean, and he asked me, "What are your feelings toward me?"

I told him the truth. I cared about him.

He said he felt the same.

The question itself felt almost unnecessary. We both knew I was leaving. We both knew the ending. And yet, we both romanticized it anyway. He told me that of all the travelers he had hosted, he had lost touch with all of them—but that he would never lose contact with me. We spoke about ideas, about possibilities, about imaginary futures.

Fantasy is easy when you don't have to live it.

I left.

He called a few times after that. Then he disappeared. No calls. No messages. Nothing.

It hurt—for a few days.

And then it didn't.

Because what that chapter gave me was not heartbreak, but precision. It reminded me that connection does not require permanence to be real, and that beauty does not need longevity to be valid. Some people enter your life not to stay, not to build, not to become your future, but to realign you with yourself. They exist to show you what still works inside you, what still responds, what still knows the truth. Maurice was not meant to remain in my life; he was meant to return me to my center. And once that happened, there was nothing left to hold onto—because I was already whole.

That chapter didn't break me. It healed me.

It showed me, once again, that my identity was intact. That my body knew the truth long before my heart tried to romanticize it. That structure matters—not just in long-term relationships, but even in fleeting ones.

And when I boarded my next flight, I didn't feel abandoned.

I felt complete.

Because I wasn't searching for someone else anymore.

I had found myself again.

Chapter 14

The Architecture of My Heart

After I came back from overseas, something in me had shifted—quietly, but in a way I could not ignore. Travel strips away distractions and hands you back a clearer version of your identity, and this time that clarity was undeniable. I finally understood what works for me and what never will.

Not long after returning, through the same traveling app I had used during my two-month reset, I decided to activate it back home. I had noticed that many locals used it as well. This time, instead of being hosted, I hosted for one night and met a lovely couple. We exchanged contacts. I was back—alive again, just me and the world—being myself, meeting friends, focusing on my career. It was the best feeling.

Then, at an event, I met someone I'll call Jack. He was harmless and light, fun to be around in a temporary kind of way, but completely meaningless in the larger context of my life. And the important part of that encounter wasn't him—it was me. For the first time, I didn't allow a misaligned connection to linger. I didn't excuse it, stretch it, or try to make it fit. I saw the red flags immediately because I finally knew myself: my structure, my emotional architecture, my nonnegotiables.

Jack moved through life with a lighter rhythm than mine—more fluid, more spontaneous, less anchored in direction. There was nothing wrong with that; it simply didn't fit the structure I require in a partner. The chivalry was charming, the spontaneity momentarily engaging, but none of it could compensate for a foundation that didn't align with my own.

What mattered in that encounter wasn't him, but me. For the first time, I didn't linger in misalignment. I didn't excuse it, stretch it, or try to make it work. I recognized the mismatch immediately and ended it cleanly, without drama or delay. That was the proof: I finally knew my structure well enough to honor it.

Around the same time, I was handling a business deal. The person working with me on that deal—let's call him Derek—was someone I had met a year earlier through business. We had lost touch for a while, until I brought clients who needed his services. By then, I was overseas on a personal retreat, managing documents between time zones, rediscovering my rhythm and my solitude.

Derek started asking about my travels, intrigued by the way I moved through the world. He had a spontaneous, adventurous spirit that made our conversations longer. I was doing what I do best— traveling alone, expanding, living freely—and I could sense his admiration, the way many people admire that kind of freedom. But admiration has never meant alignment.

As we continued talking, subtle truths began to surface: his emotional reliance on family, the way he blended his world with others, and the way his life structure operated in a rhythm different from mine. None of it was wrong. It simply wasn't for me. He was living a life that worked for him, but one I could never fit into without betraying my identity.

At that moment, there wasn't even a remote thought that he would enter my life romantically—that idea was completely out of reality. The reason I describe what I observed is because I noticed these red flags for my structure even when I wasn't thinking of him romantically at all. Even as friends, some of it felt disruptive, slightly irritating, misaligned.

Still, he became very important in my life, and I will speak more about that later.

Around this period, I also had a conversation with someone who lives in a completely different relationship structure than I do— someone whose world naturally involves blending and extended family dynamics. And yet, she understood me instantly. She didn't dismiss my standards or call them extreme. Instead, she recognized that a person who truly knows themselves can understand identities different from their own without judgment.

That moment showed me something important: people who react negatively to the way I love are reflecting their own limits, not mine. Judgment is projection. It is a mirror of fears, insecurities, and unfulfilled strengths. People judge what they are unable to imagine for themselves. They judge what they cannot do. They judge where they feel weak. But people who are secure in their identity don't need you to live like them for your life to make sense. They can say, *This works for me, and I understand why that works for you.* That is emotional intelligence. That is maturity.

What I require in love—a partner-first bond, a private and sovereign relationship space, a deep unity without external interference—is not common. But rare does not mean unreasonable. Rare simply means specific. And specific women require specific men.

Clarity is not rigidity. Clarity is self-knowledge.

The moment I understood that, everything in my life aligned. I am not for everyone, and I am not meant to be. I don't need the world to adopt my structure. I only need the right person to respect it—and the right person won't just respect it, he will match it.

Because when you know who you are and what your love is built for, misalignment stops being painful. It becomes obvious. And endings become clean steps toward the life you are designed to live.

Chapter 15

When Clarity Replaces Curiosity

Now let's get back to Derek.

Derek and I met on social media while I was networking for my business. This was months before Dylan ever entered the picture. At the time, my life was oriented toward growth, expansion, and building something meaningful, and I used social platforms primarily as tools for connection and professional alignment. Derek reached out because he was visiting Nashville from Ohio and wanted to network in the area. Our conversations online were engaging and intelligent, grounded in business and shared curiosity, and although we never even spoke on the phone, there was enough substance for me to agree to meet him in person.

I met him at a bar lounge near my house. As always, I was careful. I didn't know him, and I trust discernment more than instinct. The conversation itself was pleasant—nothing dramatic, nothing rushed, simply two people talking comfortably. We agreed to meet again the next day because I had a business partner at the time and wanted to introduce them. That second meeting took place at a distillery, with plans to later move to another location to meet my partner.

It was during that first evening that I casually mentioned I had a dating app, not with intention or strategy, but openly, the way I speak when I am not hiding anything. I talked freely about my life, about being open to meeting someone someday, about curiosity rather than expectation. At that time, Dylan was not even a presence in my world. Derek remained respectful throughout—no overt advances, no pressure, no crossed lines. Still, I sensed something subtle, an attraction perhaps, but it was unverified and unspoken, and I never move based on assumption.

We later met my business partner at a venue with live music. We spent time there, talked, listened, and eventually decided to continue the evening elsewhere. My business partner wanted a place halfway between her town and mine, which limited options, and after a couple of quiet stops and a few drinks, she decided to call it a night. The evening ended naturally. No expectations, no tension, just a completed moment.

The next day, I had a podcast scheduled with Derek—an online interview focused entirely on business. I wanted to highlight his work and add it to my professional portfolio. Around that time, I also had a client who needed his services. That case turned out to be complex, and we eventually had to pause it until the client gathered additional documentation. After that, we didn't speak much for months.

When the client was finally ready, I reached out again. By then, Dylan had entered my life, and although that relationship was not even official—we were barely two weeks into seeing each other— there was already jealousy around Derek. Still, this was business, and my priority has always been serving my clients with integrity. We completed the work successfully, and once the case closed, I stepped back from further communication to avoid unnecessary complications. Derek was not the only professional I could work with, and at that moment, keeping my personal life simple mattered more.

Months later, everything shifted.

I was about to leave for my two-month reset overseas—the same trip that followed the collapse with Dylan. Right before leaving, I had another client, but the person assisting with that file was not responsive. Dylan was no longer in my life, and Derek had already proven reliable in difficult cases, so I reached out again. The clients still weren't fully ready, but we began organizing their files, and then I left for my trip.

While I was overseas, Derek and I spoke more frequently. Some of it was business, but naturally, conversations expanded. He asked about my travels, my experiences, and the places I was visiting. I was alone, grounded, and deeply reconnected with myself, and I could sense admiration in the way he listened. But admiration has never been the same as alignment for me, and I've learned not to confuse the two.

When I returned home, it was time to finalize the deal. Derek decided to come to Nashville to meet the clients in person. He initially planned to rent an Airbnb, as he had before, but I offered him my extra room instead. It was a simple act of practicality and kindness. There was no hidden meaning behind it, and he never crossed a line. He remained respectful at all times.

Over the course of two or three visits—each tied to closing the case—we spent time talking in my living room. During the last visit, he tested proximity, rubbing my feet lightly, and I immediately pulled back. It was subtle, but clear. I didn't react emotionally; I reacted structurally. He was testing the waters, and I was setting boundaries. He didn't push further.

Around that time, I was briefly seeing someone else. I was transparent about it with Derek, not out of provocation, but because honesty felt natural between us. I didn't hide my dating life, nor did I dramatize it. In that phase, Derek had become more of a confidant than anything else—a steady presence, a safe conversational space, someone I trusted enough to speak freely with. After that night, he didn't push for anything more. Weeks passed without him trying again, and the dynamic settled quietly back into its familiar rhythm.

But clarity has a way of revealing itself fully when you already know who you are.

Even if physical attraction had existed—which it didn't at the time—the structural misalignment was unmistakable. Derek's life was still deeply intertwined with a previous chapter, one that remained active, influential, and emotionally present in his everyday world. For someone like me, whose identity is rooted in sovereignty, emotional independence, and a partner-centered structure, that kind of configuration is not something I can step into without losing my sense of sanctuary. I am not built to blend lives that are still orbiting former dynamics. I am built to build forward—cleanly, intentionally, and without divided time or emotional residue. What worked for him was not wrong; it simply contradicted the life I have consciously and carefully designed.

This is not about people. It has never been about people. It is about structure.

I am not built for relationships where the past remains an active force in the present. I need a partnership anchored in emotional autonomy, resolution, and forward momentum—where what we are building together is primary, not secondary. When a relationship requires constant accommodation of earlier structures or unresolved ties, it places me in a visiting role rather than a foundational one. And I have always known I am not meant to live that way.

Everyone has their own identity, their own structure, their own way of inhabiting love. The point is not to change one another, persuade one another, or negotiate cores that were never meant to bend. The point is to stay grounded in who you are, to live fully where you belong, and to allow others to live fully where *they* belong—without resentment, without guilt, and without distortion. Structure does not change easily, because it is not a preference; it is part of the core. And when two structures do not align, the most honest act is not compromise, but clarity. Love does not require self-erasure to be real. It requires truth. The work is not to adapt yourself into someone else's world, but to recognize where you fit naturally—and to choose a partner whose identity aligns with yours, without forcing either one of you to become something you are not.

In my architecture, I am not a guest. I am the center.

Blended structures, constant family orbiting, emotional dependence disguised as closeness—those are not compatible with the life I have protected for decades. This is not judgment. This is self-knowledge. And self-knowledge requires boundaries that do not apologize for existing.

This time was different from all the others. I didn't debate. I didn't justify. I didn't second-guess. I didn't try to make something fit.

I saw clearly what I would never allow into my life, and I honored that clarity without drama. That is what growth looks like. That is what healing becomes. That is what identity does when it is no longer negotiable.

Derek was never my type physically, and I recognized that early on. But more than attraction, I pay attention to patterns. I observe before I engage. Even without romantic interest, I could already sense the ways our lives moved at different rhythms—the subtle misalignments in structure, pace, and orientation that would eventually surface. It wasn't dramatic or confusing; it was quiet and clear. A simple inner knowing that this was not something meant to be pursued.

What surprised me instead was how close we became as friends. Derek was an excellent confidant. Our conversations grew more frequent and more personal, and in a season when I was overwhelmed—especially with business—I found comfort in being able to speak openly to someone who listened without judgment. One day, when I was carrying too much and felt emotionally exhausted, he called me just to check in. His kindness was gentle, uncomplicated. It felt good to cry in front of someone without having to explain myself.

That was when he offered to host me in his hometown. Not as pressure, not as expectation—just an invitation to get out of my head for a night. He rented an Airbnb. During the day, we spent time together, talked, went out, and had drinks. He was attentive and caring, and I felt genuinely supported. That night, when we returned to the Airbnb, he instinctively took the couch while I went to bed. Something about that restraint moved me. I told him he didn't have to stay on the couch. One thing led to another, and I allowed the moment to unfold.

I was clear with myself even then: whatever happened that night was not a story I wanted to continue or dissect. I did not want it to turn into meaning or memory. I wanted no conversation the next day, no emotional extension, no narrative attached. I knew exactly why. His life structure was incompatible with mine, and attachment would have been a betrayal of my identity.

I am a passionate woman, fully embodied in my femininity, and I won't deny that the physical experience itself was intense—unexpectedly so. But intensity has never been my measure of alignment. The next morning, I pulled back immediately, without drama, without explanation. Not out of shame, but out of clarity.

What that moment taught me mattered more than the moment itself. It confirmed something essential: chemistry does not override structure. Comfort does not equal compatibility. And just because something feels good does not mean it belongs in your life.

I wanted to avoid attachment not because I was confused, but because I was certain. His life would have been a tornado inside mine, and I have spent too many years building an architecture that does not survive chaos. Knowing when to stop—even after pleasure—is not detachment. It is self-respect.

And more than anything, it confirmed that I finally knew who I was.

But clarity does not always end a story immediately. Derek moved closer than I expected, and what followed became far more complicated than I had intended.

Chapter 16

Identity Is Not Negotiable

Derek didn't push, but he stayed. And slowly, almost without me noticing, he moved closer. I played with fire knowingly, and the danger was never desire—it was attachment. We had built a strong friendship first, one grounded in conversation, trust, and emotional safety. I confided in him freely, without filters or defenses. He listened. He held space. He showed up in the ways that felt natural to him. He also shared my love for travel, and that created a sense of resonance—something light, familiar, and easy to step into.

But even then, I knew the risk. Even attempting something casual threatened the friendship itself. A serious relationship was never on the table—not because of fear, but because of clarity. Entering a committed partnership with him would have hurt me by default, not by intention, and that was the hardest truth to sit with. I didn't want to lose the friendship, yet I had already crossed a boundary that complicated everything. I don't deny that I enjoyed the closeness. There was real connection, undeniable chemistry, and something that in its way was love—except for the one thing that mattered most: alignment.

I tried, more than once, to explain this to him. I told him that love alone was never enough for me. That I don't measure love by connection only—I measure it by structure. I told him that the natural behaviors of his life structure would eventually wreck me emotionally, even if he never meant to hurt me. He would hurt me by default, simply by being who he was, and that would inevitably lead to resentment on both sides. Still, it moved forward. And I tried, foolishly perhaps, to ignore what I already knew.

I went along silently. I treated it as something casual, hoping that distance would soften the attachment, especially since we didn't even live in the same state. I used that separation as a buffer, convincing myself that things might fade on their own. But when he visited again, and I invited him to an event with friends, the closeness deepened instead. I felt it clearly—this needed to end. Yet there were practical entanglements now. Business was involved. My clients had already spoken with him, and even though not everything was official, it felt unprofessional and unfair to disrupt that simply because of personal boundaries.

And the truth is, Derek was perfect in many ways. Kind. Present. Consistent. Everything was there—except the structure. And breaking my structure is non-negotiable for me, not out of stubbornness, but out of clarity.

I often explain it this way: some women know, without question, that motherhood is their core identity. They thrive in it. It is essential to know who they are. If that woman enters a relationship with a man who does not want children, no amount of love will fix that misalignment. She might compromise. He might hope it won't matter. But eventually, it resurfaces as resentment, grief, or loss of self. Identity cannot be negotiated without consequence.

That was the situation here. Derek believed that emotional closeness would soften me, that if he showed enough care, consistency, and affection, I would adapt. But this wasn't about softness—it was about wiring. I knew it. Explaining my structure felt irrelevant, because structure isn't a preference; it's a system. It's like a man trying to convince a woman she doesn't need children, saying, *Why do you need that? You have me. I love you. I'm here.* And yet, that is not enough. Collapse is inevitable.

He asked me many times, *What can I do?* as if this were something actionable, something teachable. But if I have to explain how a man needs to show up for me to feel emotionally safe, then he is not the man.

Put simply, there are people whose identity is rooted in a calling. Not a job, not a phase, but a life orientation. Artists, founders, researchers, surgeons, writers—people who organize their lives around creation, discipline, and long periods of focus. If such a person partners with someone who needs constant availability, predictability, or emotional presence to feel secure, no amount of love will resolve the conflict. They may try to adjust. They may promise balance. They may compromise temporarily. But eventually, tension resurfaces—not because either person is wrong, but because a calling cannot be diluted without eroding the self.

That kind of misalignment doesn't announce itself as danger in the beginning. It shows up later, as resentment, exhaustion, or a quiet grief that has no language. And by the time it appears, it has already cost both people something irreplaceable.

My structure works the same way. What destabilizes me may be neutral or even beautiful to someone else, but neutrality does not equal alignment. Love does not cancel architecture. Emotional closeness does not override identity. When someone's life naturally bleeds into mine, not through intention but through default, I know—without anger, without drama—that I am no longer safe inside myself.

Still, during the time I hoped things would naturally fade, a trip was approaching. I always plan my solo travels, and I was going overseas for my birthday, as always.. He had often expressed how much he wanted to join me on one of my trips, and eventually, I invited him. I knew the reality, but our connection was the best I had ever experienced; it felt irreplaceable. And because I was still grounded and not committing, I believed I could handle it. To me, it felt harmless. I have always enjoyed traveling with companions.

But deep inside, I already knew I was attached, even while my mind tried to pretend otherwise.

The connection was deep, one of the deepest of my life. When I say connection, I mean something free, expansive, and emotionally intimate. I felt like myself with him, except in the moments when he triggered me by default, simply because we were wired differently.

While overseas, everything was beautiful—except for one thing. His life bled into mine constantly. I never expressed commitment. I was always clear: I am not committing to anything. That was my unconscious way of saying goodbye without drama, without cruelty, without forcing a rupture. But the constant calls, the emotional spillover, the presence of his past entering my structure—it invaded the very space I use to disconnect, regulate, and return to myself.

My trips are sacred. They are where I reset my nervous system, where my life goes quiet. And there, even in public moments, seeing elements of a life I did not choose surface in ways I couldn't control made something painfully clear to me. In my structure, everything must be contained. Private. Intentional. Sacred. I could never be emotionally safe with him like that.

And this is where the chapter pauses—not with blame, not with certainty, but with truth.

Some people can restructure their lives. But they must do it because they feel called to live that way—not because they are trying to hold onto someone. Identity cannot be borrowed. Structure cannot be performed. And it is never my responsibility to wait, hope, or bend who I am so someone else can catch up.

I will never bend my architecture.

What became increasingly clear to me was that Derek understood calibration as adjustment—small gestures, reassurances, effort made in my direction. But what I was speaking about lived much deeper than behavior. True alignment, for someone like me, requires restructuring—not for another person, but for oneself. The question was never whether he cared for me or wanted to meet me where I stood. The question was whether he could inhabit that way of living even if I were not there to witness it.

Could he organize his inner world around a chosen partnership as the primary axis of his life—emotionally, energetically, and practically—so that nothing else diluted that center? Not as an act of exclusion, but as an act of clarity. Because a real partnership does not ask to be fitted in; it asks to be placed first.

And the truth is, for most people, the answer is no—not because they are incapable or flawed, but because their identity is built differently. That way of living carries a cost. It asks for solitude, containment, and a level of internal authority that not everyone desires or needs. Both structures are valid. But they are fundamentally different.

This is what I mean by restructuring. It is not about changing for love. It is about whether the life you are being asked to inhabit is one you would choose even in the absence of that love. Anything else eventually becomes resentment—not because anyone is wrong, but because identity cannot be borrowed without consequence.

Whether Derek could ever truly live within it—without sacrificing himself, without resentment, without imitation—was not a question I needed answered.

Because if love requires me to become smaller, quieter, or less precise about who I am, then love is not the answer.

And so what remained was not a decision to be made, but a truth already standing. Some people can restructure their lives, yes — but only when that restructuring is born from internal conviction, not from proximity, desire, or fear of loss. Architecture that lasts is never adopted for someone else; it is claimed because it feels inevitable.

What I had awakened in him, if anything, was never mine to manage. Awareness does not guarantee transformation, and transformation does not erase cost. To live within my structure would require more than adjustment — it would require reverence. Not accommodation. Not negotiation. Reverence for the center of my life as it already exists.

In my world, entry into my life is not automatic—especially when it involves bonds that predate the partnership and extend beyond it.

Access, if I ever choose to allow it, is earned, not assumed. Respect must come before proximity. I do not adapt my rhythm, my time, or my structure to accommodate disruption. A queen's life is not rearranged; it is honored. Those who enter my world do so understanding the hierarchy: I am not secondary, I am not supplemental, and I am not waiting to be fit in. I am the center from which the family is built. I arrive first, I am considered first, and I am protected first—not out of dominance, but out of order. And those who truly belong will recognize that instinctively, not challenge it.

And at the same time, I knew.

I knew that if I stayed, his structure would continue to bleed into mine. I knew that resentment would eventually take root—not because he was wrong, but because I would be betraying myself. And for a sovereign woman, that kind of self-betrayal is not dramatic; it is corrosive.

Why would I place myself in that position? Why would I place him there? You do not borrow another person's identity in order to live your own. That is not fair to either side. That is what I refused to do with Derek.

What was possible between us did not disappear. The connection was real. The love was real. But connection alone cannot carry a structure it was never designed to hold.

Whether he could ever live inside the architecture I require—naturally, independently, without effort or performance—was not a question I needed to answer. And it was not a question I needed to wait on.

My responsibility was not to close anything, nor to keep anything open. My responsibility was to remain intact.

Some paths only reveal themselves when both people arrive whole, without persuasion, without accommodation, without cost to themselves.

Until then, I remain exactly where I am—rooted in my identity, unattached to outcome, and loyal to the life I have built.

Chapter 17

A Sovereign Woman Does Not Blend

Most people move through love the way travelers move through airports—following signs, following crowds, following whichever gate feels closest. They make choices from emotion, attachment, and the fear of being alone. They stay because it feels familiar, because it feels good enough, because someone is kind or present. They blend into lives without ever asking whether those lives were meant to hold them.

I learned something different about myself.

I never dated based on emotion. I dated from instinct—long before I had the language to understand what that meant.

Before clarity settled into my bones, before identity became something I could name, I still knew. I didn't yet understand my architecture, but my body did. I didn't know I was sovereign, that I was meant to be the core of a relationship rather than an addition to someone else's world, but something in me already refused what didn't fit. Even without words, my intuition protected me.

While others adjusted, explained, compromised, or blended, something in me quietly stepped back. Something in me said no—even when the man was gentle, emotionally available, or offering a future. Something in me recognized that misalignment does not become alignment simply because affection is present.

That instinct saved my life.

Most people don't leave when everything looks good on paper. Most people don't walk away from kind men or women who are chaotic. Most people don't say, "This is good—but it is not mine." I did, even when I couldn't explain why.

I didn't have the vocabulary yet. I didn't have psychological clarity. But my nervous system recognized misalignment years before my mind could name it. That is why I never stayed with men who lacked structure. That is why I never blended into families where I didn't belong. That is why I never built a life that required me to abandon myself. My intuition was my architect, while my identity was still under construction.

People often ask why I didn't become a mother earlier. The answer is simple: because my instinct said not with him—and not yet. If I had chosen motherhood with the men I dated before fully knowing myself, I would have raised a child inside misalignment, tied forever to a structure that could not hold me. My soul knew that. My life unfolded accordingly.

This is where many people misunderstand me. They hear words like *standards*, *structure*, and *boundaries* and assume rigidity, fear, or control. But clarity is not rigidity, and boundaries are not punishments. They are information.

People talk endlessly about compromise. For me, compromise is not the work. **Calibration** is.

Compromise asks you to sacrifice parts of yourself to maintain peace. Calibration asks you to adjust behavior while preserving identity. The difference is everything.

A person whose identity is rooted in building—creating, expanding, taking risks, moving forward—cannot calibrate themselves into fulfillment with a partner whose deepest need is stability, routine, and predictability. They can slow down. They can reassure. They can promise to stay put. But eventually, the tension resurfaces—not because either person is wrong, but because one is forced to live against their nature. Identity does not disappear simply because love asks it to.

What I require in love—a partner-first bond, a private and sovereign relationship space, unity without external interference—is not common. But rare does not mean unreasonable. Rare means specific. And specific women require specific men.

Some women thrive in blended families, emotional merging, and extended closeness. That life fits their identity. Mine requires something else: a man who stands on his own, who leads with structure, who protects the relationship as its own universe, who does not ask me to bend my architecture to accommodate his past.

This does not make me cold. It makes me clear.

I am not rejecting people. I am protecting the center of my life.

What I share here is my experience—how I found myself, how loyal I became to my identity, how respect for myself became nonnegotiable. This is mine. Whatever yours is, *that* is what will guide you. You do not need the world's approval to be fulfilled. You need alignment with the right people. You do not want someone to win you. You want someone to match you.

Connection is beautiful. Emotion is beautiful. Desire is beautiful. But without structure, they are fireworks—brilliant and temporary. Alignment stays. Structure stays. Identity stays for as long as you live.

Yes, people can restructure. But true restructuring never happens because someone wants to keep another person. It happens because they recognize themselves in the mirror and choose that truth independently. Identity cannot be borrowed. It must be inhabited.

I did not fail at relationships. I was not left behind. I was being shaped, protected, and prepared—for love with architecture, not chaos; for alignment, not attachment.

There comes a moment in a woman's evolution when the life she built becomes her clearest mirror. Not the life she came from. Not the life she escaped. But the life she built with her own hands. In that moment, she understands something most people never articulate: a partner must be able to hold the life she created—or she will betray herself by choosing them.

Affection is not architecture.

Kindness is not alignment.

Desire is not capacity.

When a woman becomes herself through resilience and independence, she does not blend. She does not shrink. She does not abandon the identity she fought for. She chooses from truth, not fear.

There is a moment in a woman's life when clarity replaces tolerance.

Not because she becomes colder.

Not because she fears love.

But because she finally understands the cost of living without structure.

For a long time, I believed something was wrong with me because I did not love the way others did. I did not crave constant reassurance. I did not feel safer by blending lives or merging systems. I did not long to be folded into preexisting worlds. What grounded me was something quieter, more internal—clarity, containment, and authorship over my own life.

It took years to understand why.

My sense of safety never came from people. It came from selfcontainment. From solitude. From movement. From choosing my life rather than inheriting it. Travel, independence, long stretches of being alone—these were not escapes for me. They were regulation. They were how my nervous system stayed intact.

Where others learned to stabilize through closeness, I learned to stabilize through order.

This did not make me detached. It made me precise.

Over time, I began to notice a pattern. Relationships did not end because they were unloving or unkind. They ended because something essential in me began to erode. My inner quiet disappeared. My sense of authorship weakened. My structure—carefully built over years—started to blur.

I learned the hard way that love without structure does not feel romantic to me.

It feels like erosion.

That realization changes everything.

Some people experience closeness as safety. Others experience it as intrusion. Neither is wrong. They are simply different orientations. My identity is built around sovereignty—emotional independence, privacy, and a clearly defined center. When someone's life naturally bleeds into mine without intention or containment, my system reacts long before my mind can explain why.

This is not judgment.

It is information.

I am not anti-family.

I am pro-order.

I am not rejecting people.

I am protecting the center of my life.

Family systems, emotional blending, inherited obligations— these work beautifully for people whose identities are built that way. Mine is not. My life is authored, not inherited. Chosen, not absorbed. And anything that asks me to become a visitor in my own life—even gently, even lovingly—is not compatible with how I stay whole.

This clarity did not arrive suddenly. It was earned through repetition. Through leaving when something looked good on paper but felt wrong in my body. Through choosing solitude over slow self-betrayal. Through learning that peace matters more to me than belonging.

That is why my structure feels strict to those who do not live it.

Strictness is what clarity looks like after experience.

It is what remains when ambiguity is no longer an option.

I do not require others to live the way I live. I do not need the world to adopt my structure. I only need alignment from the person who enters my life most closely. And alignment does not mean effort or adjustment—it means recognition. It means a man whose life already moves with the same containment, whose center is already clear, whose peace does not depend on proximity, validation, or inherited systems.

Rare does not mean unreasonable.

Rare means specific.

And specific women require specific men.

This is not about being difficult.

It is about being loyal.

When a woman finally understands what breaks her and what sustains her, she stops negotiating her architecture. Not out of fear—but out of self-respect. She does not ask to be accommodated. She does not soften what is essential. She simply remains intact.

And that is not the absence of love.

That is the foundation of the only kind of love that can last for her.

This principle is not exclusive to women. Anyone who has built a life through clarity, effort, and self-respect reaches this same threshold. Identity becomes non-negotiable. Alignment becomes the filter.

Some may call this way of living too strong, too defined, too much. But this is my identity, and I am clear about it. Not every woman—or every person—is meant to live this way, and that is perfectly okay. There is no hierarchy here. Only alignment.

Know who you are first.

Then you filter—not date.

You choose from identity, not loneliness.

That is how lasting love is built.

It begins with you.

Always you.

Chapter 18

Identity-Based Love

For a long time, I believed something was wrong with me because I did not love the way people expected me to. I did not need constant reassurance; I needed actions, wholeness, someone ready to share a life with me. I never felt safer by merging my life into someone else's. Intimacy, for me, did not grow louder with more access, more visibility, more people involved. What grounded me was the opposite. What made me feel secure was clarity, structure, and a clearly defined center.

And yet, this creates a challenge. How do you love someone whose structure is based on blending when you have worked diligently to build a sovereign life? How do you share a life without betraying yourself? That kind of betrayal does not disappear—it eventually explodes. We cannot lie to ourselves by believing we can change others to fit our lives, or that love and connection will cure everything, when our nervous system is already reacting. When your body knows, you must listen. You must walk toward peace, whatever that looks like for you. Loving yourself has to come first.

At first, I thought this was emotional distance. Later, I understood it was emotional sovereignty.

Most love stories are built on attachment. Attachment-based love bonds through proximity, reassurance, shared wounds, and the fear of loss. It grows by accumulation: more time together, more access, more sharing, more blending. For many people, this works. For many people, attachment *is* safety. But we must be careful here. Attachment can be intense, filled with fireworks, and detaching can hurt deeply. This is precisely why people who rely on identity-based love rather than attachment-based love scan the architecture first— to make sure the relationship can last.

Think of this scenario, and I am not saying everyone lives this way, but I have seen it many times, and I have lived it myself. People get together, start a relationship, or even get married, because the connection feels amazing. "We can talk for hours. This feels right. I love this person." But what about goals? Ambitions? Daily actions? Priorities? Are those aligned? If they are not, compromise enters quietly. And the realization may come months later—or years later—depending on how much you are willing to carry.

Some people get married because of an unexpected pregnancy. But did they ask the real questions? Will this person be a good parent? Do we share parenting values? Do we share long-term goals? Now alignment is forced instead of chosen. Restructuring is not adjustable. It is rooted in who you are. And when people enter relationships without considering architecture, they live inside a question mark: *Does this structure align with mine or not?*

Sometimes it works. Often it doesn't.

The process can be long—misunderstandings, arguments, resentment. You either compromise and live incomplete, or you leave, now tied to someone forever if children are involved, carrying a chapter you cannot undo into the next life you actually wanted. This is what identity-based love avoids from the beginning. Not because it is better—but because it requires strength. It requires not letting emotions blur your structure.

This does not mean we do not feel. It means we prefer less time detaching painfully than a lifetime compromising what truly makes us happy. And yes, it hurts when someone does not align with you. It can feel like rejection. But the truth is simpler: that person did not have the capacity to match you. Walking away with integrity is painful, but pain passes. Self-betrayal does not.

We more often than we think believe calibration means adjusting behavior. But calibration is not the question here; restructuring is. And again, even if restructuring were possible, it is not for us to demand. That work has to be acknowledged and done alone by the other person. Someone can love, can say you are willing to adjust—

but can they live the life of a sovereign, emotionally independent without you in the picture? Can they stand alone? Can they live without constant emotional tethering, without blurred roles, without relying on proximity to regulate their sense of self? Most likely not. And that is what I mean by restructuring. Can they take the cost?

What I eventually understood is that behavior is never the problem. Behavior is simply the surface expression of structure. When two identities are aligned, the rhythms of life fall into place without negotiation. The boundaries exist without being drawn. The priorities arrange themselves without explanation. You don't ask for containment, privacy, or emotional sovereignty — it arrives naturally, because it is already how that person lives.

When alignment is absent, however, everything becomes a discussion. Every action needs context. Every pattern needs justification. Every boundary needs to be requested, reinforced, and explained. And at that point, the issue is no longer communication — it is architecture. Because structure does not respond to instruction. It only responds to truth.

A sovereign identity does not perform restraint; it embodies it. It does not regulate itself for someone else's comfort; it lives from an internal order that does not require witnesses, reminders, or external validation. And when someone's life operates from a different core, no amount of affection or intention can override that reality.

That is what I mean by restructuring. Not changing behavior for love, but living in a way that would look exactly the same even if no one were watching — even if I were not there.

Both structures are valid. Both can work for the right people. One does not make you less than the other. They are simply different— rooted in different cores.

For someone like me, attachment without structure becomes suffocating.

Identity-based love does not begin with closeness. It begins with positioning. It asks a different question—not "How much can we share?" but "What must remain protected for love to stay alive?"

This was the part I could not articulate for years. I didn't know how to explain why relationships that looked loving on the surface never settled inside me. Men arrived with affection, attention, presence, and intention. Some were kind. Some were emotionally available. Some wanted to build something real. And still, something in me resisted merging.

It was not fear. It was misalignment.

Attachment-based love assumes love deepens when lives blend. Identity-based love understands that love deepens when lives remain intact. When two people stand fully inside who they are, connection becomes stable rather than consuming.

This is why phrases like "you have to love the whole package" never resonated with me. Life is not a package. Life is a sequence. We move through phases, and emotionally mature people know how to close chapters instead of carrying them forward indefinitely. Containment is not rejection. Separation is not denial. Privacy is not coldness.

It is an intention.

I learned this not through theory, but by watching what fails. Attachment-based love fails for people like me because it asks us to override our internal architecture in order to keep the bond alive. It rewards sacrifice over alignment. It confuses endurance with devotion.

For someone whose identity is built on structure, that is not love. That is erosion.

Some people are wired to regulate life internally. They process quietly, independently, without constant emotional exchange. Others regulate through closeness—daily contact, shared processing, continuous reassurance. Neither is wrong. But when a person whose identity requires emotional sovereignty partners with someone who regulates through proximity, love does not solve the mismatch. One feels invaded. The other feels abandoned. Resentment appears not because love was missing, but because identity was negotiated.

The same is true with lifestyle. Some people are built for movement, reinvention, and long stretches of autonomy. Others are rooted in routine, familiarity, and constant presence. When these identities meet, attraction can be intense—but longevity depends on alignment. Otherwise, one person slowly feels trapped, while the other feels perpetually destabilized. Again, not because anyone failed, but because identity was ignored.

Then there is authority. Some people are sovereign by nature. They lead their lives privately, decisively, without consensus. They do not merge by default. They do not blend without intention. If such a person partners with someone who requires constant inclusion, shared authority, or emotional dependence, the tension becomes inevitable. One will shrink. The other will feel excluded. And no amount of affection can compensate for that loss of self.

Identity-based love refuses that negotiation.

It does not argue. It does not convince. It does not convert. It simply does not enter spaces where self-betrayal would be required.

This is the difference between compromise and calibration. Compromise sacrifices parts of who you are to preserve the relationship. Calibration adjusts logistics—distance, rhythm, timing—while remaining loyal to identity. You can calibrate schedules. You can calibrate geography. You cannot calibrate your nervous system. You cannot calibrate what makes you feel safe. You cannot calibrate the structure your love requires.

That is not rigidity. That is self-knowledge.

Attachment-based love often mistakes intensity for depth. Identity based love understands that depth is quiet. It does not perform. It does not rush. It does not need proof.

It waits—not out of fear, but out of certainty.

And here is the part most people misunderstand: those who react strongly against this way of loving are rarely reacting to you. They are reacting to the limits of their own identity. Secure people can witness a love structure different from their own without invalidating it. They can say, "This works for me, and I understand why that works for you."

That is emotional maturity.

Identity-based love is rare because it requires something most people never develop: a stable, honest, non-negotiable relationship with themselves. Once you know who you are, dating changes. You stop auditioning. You stop explaining. You stop negotiating your center.

You filter—not out of arrogance, but out of respect.

And when alignment appears, it does not feel dramatic. It feels calm. It feels familiar. It feels like nothing inside you needs to move out of place.

That is how you know.

Love is not universal in shape. It mirrors identity. And the partnerships that last are not built on attachment, intensity, or sacrifice, but on two people who already know who they are and choose to meet without asking the other to bend.

Before I end this chapter, I want to leave you with a mirror.

Not advice. Not instruction. Just questions.

When you imagine love, do you imagine closeness—or safety?

Do you feel more alive when lives merge—or when lives stand side by side?

Have you ever stayed because leaving felt harder than betraying yourself?
Have you ever called compromise "growth" when it was actually erosion?
Do you crave reassurance—or clarity?

And the most important question: when you are alone, do you feel incomplete—or intact?

There is no right answer. Only your answer.

Some people thrive in attachment. Others thrive in sovereignty. Some build love by blending. Others build love by protecting the center. Neither is superior. Only alignment matters.

Whatever your identity is, you must know it first. Only then can you recognize the love that fits your architecture. Because a lasting partnership is not created by winning someone over. It is created by matching.

And when you finally understand that, love stops feeling like something you chase—and starts feeling like something that arrives naturally, quietly, and without force.

It begins with you.

Always you.

Author's Note on Theory, Structure, and Identity-Based Love

This book is a memoir.

Everything shared here is lived experience—felt, endured, questioned, and integrated over time. It is not a psychology textbook, nor does it attempt to formalize a new clinical theory. What it offers instead is a deeply personal account of how I came to understand myself, my patterns, and the way I love.

Over the years, through observation, reflection, travel, and long periods of solitude, I began to recognize that the way relationships either flourished or fractured in my life was not random. Certain dynamics repeated themselves with striking consistency, regardless of place, culture, or circumstance. Long before I had language for it, my body and intuition were responding to something structural— something rooted in identity.

Only later did I discover that many of these lived patterns align closely with well-established psychological and philosophical frameworks. While I did not encounter these ideas in theory first, they later provided clarity and validation to experiences I had already lived.

Much of what I describe in this book as **identity-based love** resonates with ideas found in Jungian psychology, particularly the concept of individuation—the lifelong process of becoming oneself. This perspective emphasizes that a mature partnership is possible only when two individuals are anchored in clear, differentiated identities, rather than seeking completion through fusion or dependency.

My reflections are also informed by family systems theory, which explores emotional differentiation, boundaries, and role clarity within relationships. The recurring themes in this book—contained worlds, structural coherence, and the distinction between partnership and external systems—echo this body of work, even though I arrived at them through lived experience rather than formal study.

In addition, research on self-concept clarity—the degree to which a person knows who they are and lives consistently with that knowledge—helped me understand why certain relationships felt misaligned from the beginning, even when affection, chemistry, or shared history were present. When identity is clear, misalignment is not confusing; it is simply information.

Attachment theory also plays a role in understanding human connection, and for many people, attachment-based love works beautifully. This book does not reject that model. Instead, it explores its limits. For some individuals—particularly those whose identity is rooted in sovereignty, structure, and self-continuity—attachment alone is not sufficient. This is not a hierarchy of love styles, but a recognition that different identities require different relational architectures.

The concept of **Identity-Based Love**, as explored here, is not meant to be universal. It is one way of loving, shaped by clarity, containment, and self-knowledge. Other forms of love are equally valid for those whose identities are rooted elsewhere. The purpose of this book is not to convince or convert, but to illuminate—to offer language where there was once confusion, and to normalize the experience of people who love deeply yet refuse to abandon themselves in the process.

This work does not instruct, diagnose, or prescribe. It reflects.

If this book gives you permission to understand yourself more clearly—whether you recognize yourself in my structure or discover that yours is entirely different—then it has done what it was meant to do.

Alignment begins with knowing who you are.

Everything else follows from there.

Conclusion

The Question That Changes Everything

I don't believe there are "no people out there." I don't believe love has disappeared, nor do I believe meaningful partnership is reserved for the lucky or the rare. What I do believe is that many of us repeat the same emotional patterns while expecting different outcomes, changing faces but not structures, stories but not foundations. When relationships end over and over again, it becomes easy to blame timing, circumstances, culture, or the limitations of the other person. Yet, over time, a quieter and more uncomfortable truth emerges— one that requires honesty rather than judgment. We are the common denominator. Not as a sentence of guilt, but as a source of agency.

Patterns persist not because we are unlucky, but because something within us keeps choosing what feels familiar, even when it no longer serves us. Until we understand why we are drawn to certain dynamics, why we tolerate particular compromises, and why we confuse intensity with compatibility, we will continue to relive the same conclusions under different names. This book was never written to glorify solitude or reject love. Humans are not designed for isolation. We grow through connection, expand through partnership, and thrive when life is shared. Wanting companionship is not a weakness; it is human nature. But there is a profound difference between seeking partnership and abandoning discernment in the process.

Strength is not measured by how much you can endure. Maturity is not proven by how much you can adapt. And love is not real if it consistently requires you to override your own nature in order to survive. The work is not asking why the right person hasn't arrived yet; the work is asking who you are when you love, and what kind of structure your identity actually requires to remain whole. That question changes everything. When you understand yourself deeply, attraction becomes more honest, choices become cleaner, and relationships stop feeling like emotional negotiations. You stop chasing what excites you momentarily and begin recognizing what can sustain you over time.

Yes, it is frustrating when the person you want is not there. Yes, waiting for alignment instead of settling for proximity can feel lonely. But the answer is not resignation, and it is not cynicism. The answer is refinement. Love is not found through urgency or force; it is found through clarity. Through knowing yourself well enough to recognize what fits and what never will. This is not about becoming closed or rigid; it is about becoming precise. Precision is not coldness—it is self-respect.

You are not difficult. You are not asking for too much. You are not wrong for needing what you need. But you do carry a responsibility—to yourself first—to examine the patterns you repeat, the standards you abandon, and the places where you disappear in order to keep something alive that was never aligned to begin with. The moment you stop asking where the right person is and start asking who you are, the entire narrative shifts. Love stops feeling scarce. It stops feeling like something to chase or prove. It becomes something you recognize when it appears.

Love is not missing. It is waiting for you to meet yourself fully. And when you do, partnership stops being a search and becomes what it was always meant to be: a recognition of alignment, not a rescue from loneliness.

There is also another truth we rarely acknowledge: not all identities are fully awake when we begin loving. Some parts of who we are remain dormant for years, softened by familiarity, comfort, social expectations, or the safety of patterns we never questioned. We learn how to belong long before we learn how to listen to ourselves. And then, sometimes, someone enters our life not to stay, but to mirror something we had forgotten was there. A version of us that we never allowed space to live. A truth that surprises even us.

That awakening can feel destabilizing. You may look at your past choices and wonder how you lived so long without knowing this part of yourself existed. You may feel guilt for wanting something different now, or confusion about why what once worked suddenly no longer does. But awakening is not betrayal. It is honesty arriving at a later time, not wrongdoing arriving at all.

The work is not deciding whether your identity has always been this way or whether it emerged over time. The work honors what is real now. Whether your identity has been alive from the beginning or dormant for decades, it deserves respect. It deserves to be lived without apology. Because in the end, the person you will live with forever is not the partner you choose—it is yourself. And abandoning that truth out of fear, loyalty to the past, or the comfort of the familiar is the quietest form of self-erasure.

If you are fortunate enough to meet someone who reflects your true self back to you—clearly, honestly, without distortion—that person may or may not remain in your life. But what they awaken must be because the version of you that finally recognizes yourself is the only one capable of choosing real alignment. And if you ever find the person who can stand beside that version of you—not threatened by it, not requiring it to shrink, not asking it to soften its edges— then you will know. Not because it feels dramatic, but because it feels steady.

Until then, pursue yourself fully. Live your identity without guilt. Whether it has been waiting quietly or standing loudly all along, it is the truest guide you have. And honoring it is not what separates you from love—it is what leads you directly to it.

About the Author

Zhara York is a writer, traveler, educator, and entrepreneur whose work explores identity, sovereignty, and the architecture of a life built with intention. She is the author of *The Traveler's Guide to Life*, the first book in *The Traveler's Guide* series, released in October 2025. *The Traveler's Guide to Love* is the second book in the series and continues the exploration of selfhood, alignment, and partnership through lived experience rather than theory.

Zhara has spent over fifteen years as an educator, licensed in both New York and Tennessee, working with diverse communities across academic and professional settings. Teaching has always been central to her identity—not only in classrooms, but in the way she approaches life, travel, and human connection. Education, for her, is not about instruction, but about clarity.

In addition to her writing, Zhara is a licensed real estate consultant in the Nashville area and a licensed financial professional. Her work focuses on helping clients understand themselves through their decisions—particularly in real estate, finances, and long-term planning. She believes that wealth, like love, requires structure, self-knowledge, and alignment.

She is also the founder of **BizNet**, an emerging real estate and business platform designed to connect people, simplify complex real estate processes, and create a more intentional, educational approach to building and investing. BizNet is currently in development and reflects the same philosophy that underpins her writing: clarity over chaos, structure over noise, and purpose over speed. Travel has been both her classroom and her mirror. Having lived across countries and cultures, often building her life from the ground up, Zhara's work is shaped by movement, independence, and deep self-observation. She does not write to persuade or prescribe, but to illuminate patterns—especially those that surface when love, ambition, and identity intersect. *The Traveler's Guide* series is not about finding someone else. It is about finding oneself—and choosing from that place.

Zhara continues to write, teach, build, and travel, guided by one enduring principle: **home is not a place, but a state of being.**